THIS BOOK BELONG TO

Name:........................

....

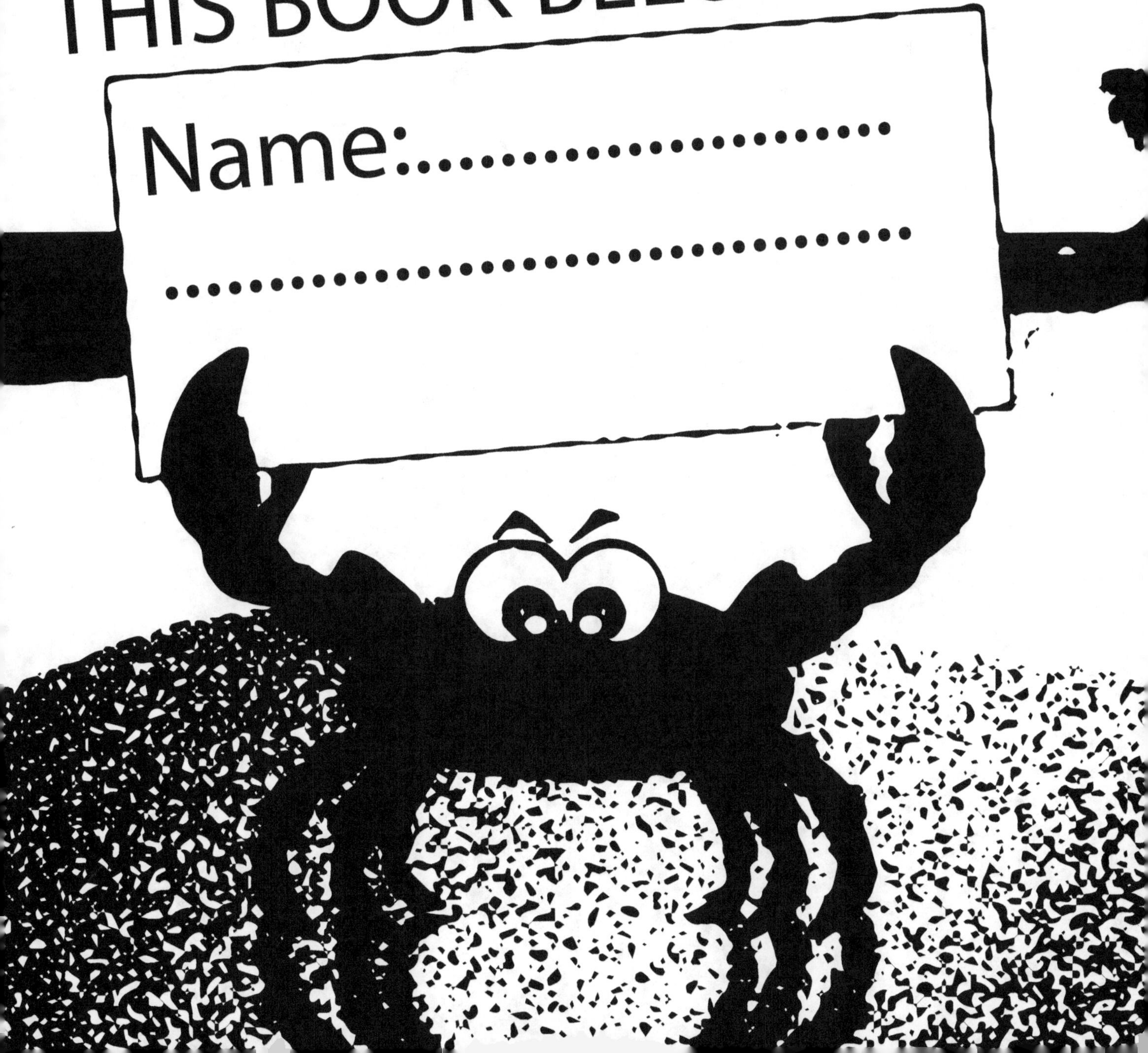

Thanks for buy a copy.
This book is for you.
Enjoy it and share.

Relax and paint in your daily life.

Dedicated to all the people who love to paint different things.

Please, leaves us a review.

ARTHUR LITTLE

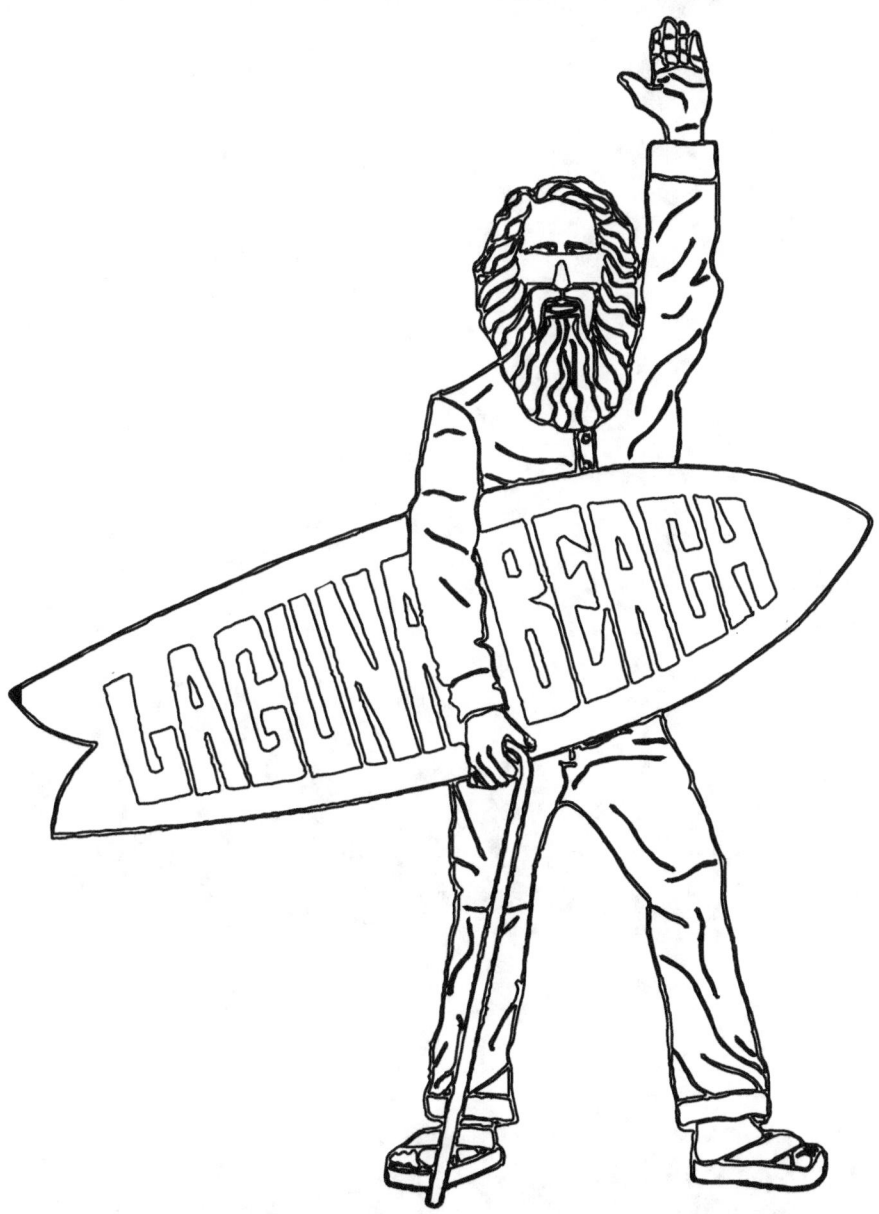

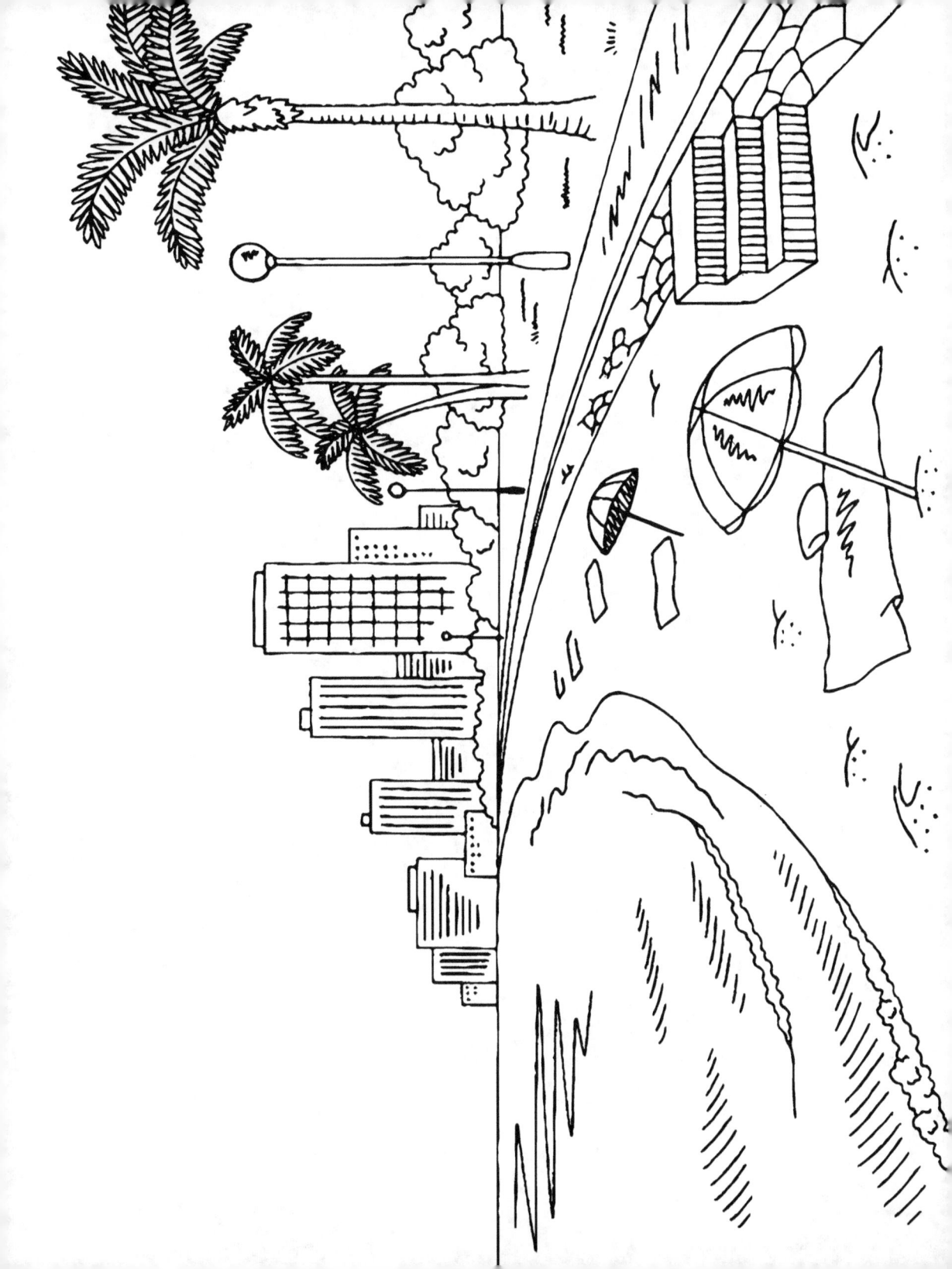

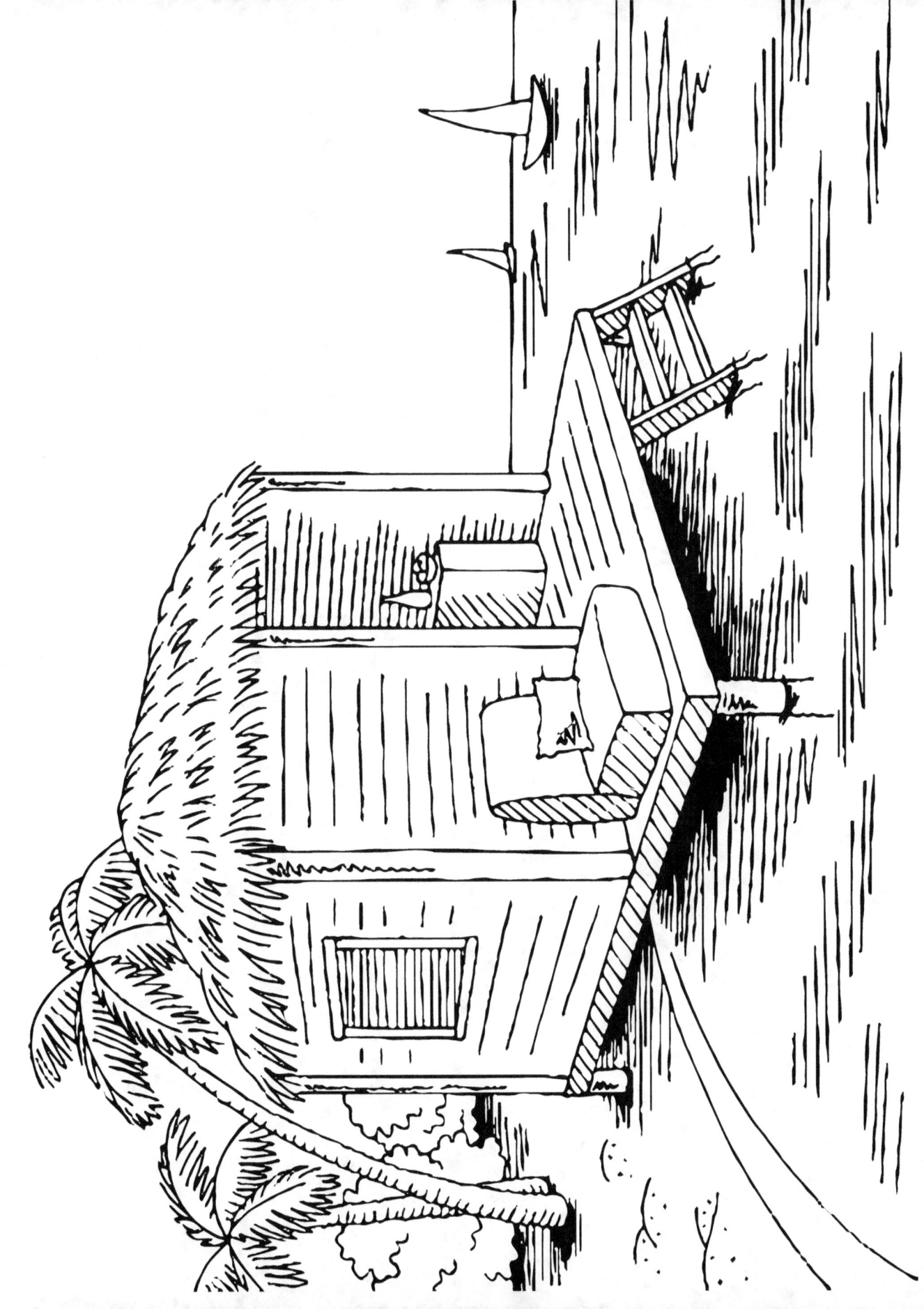

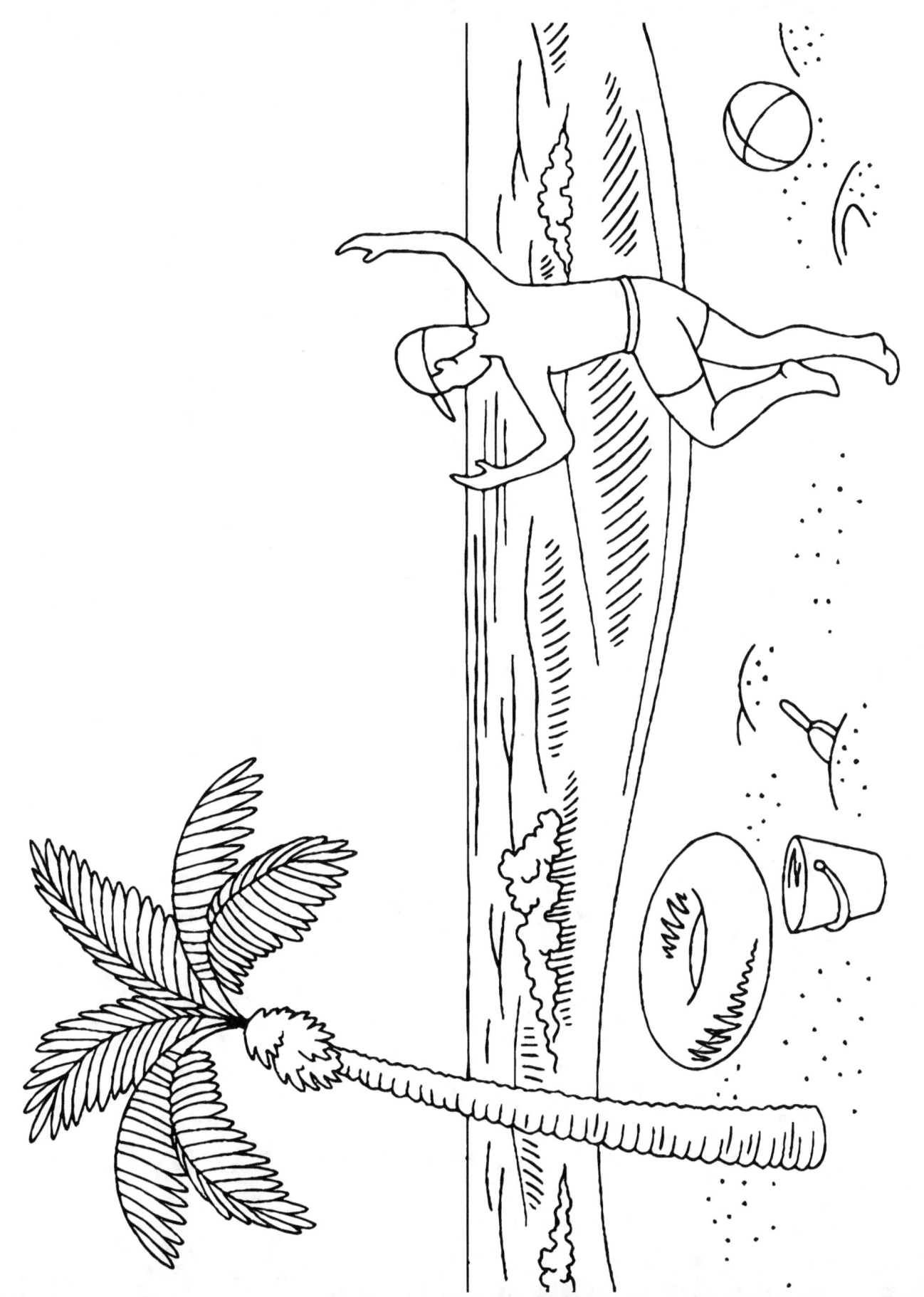

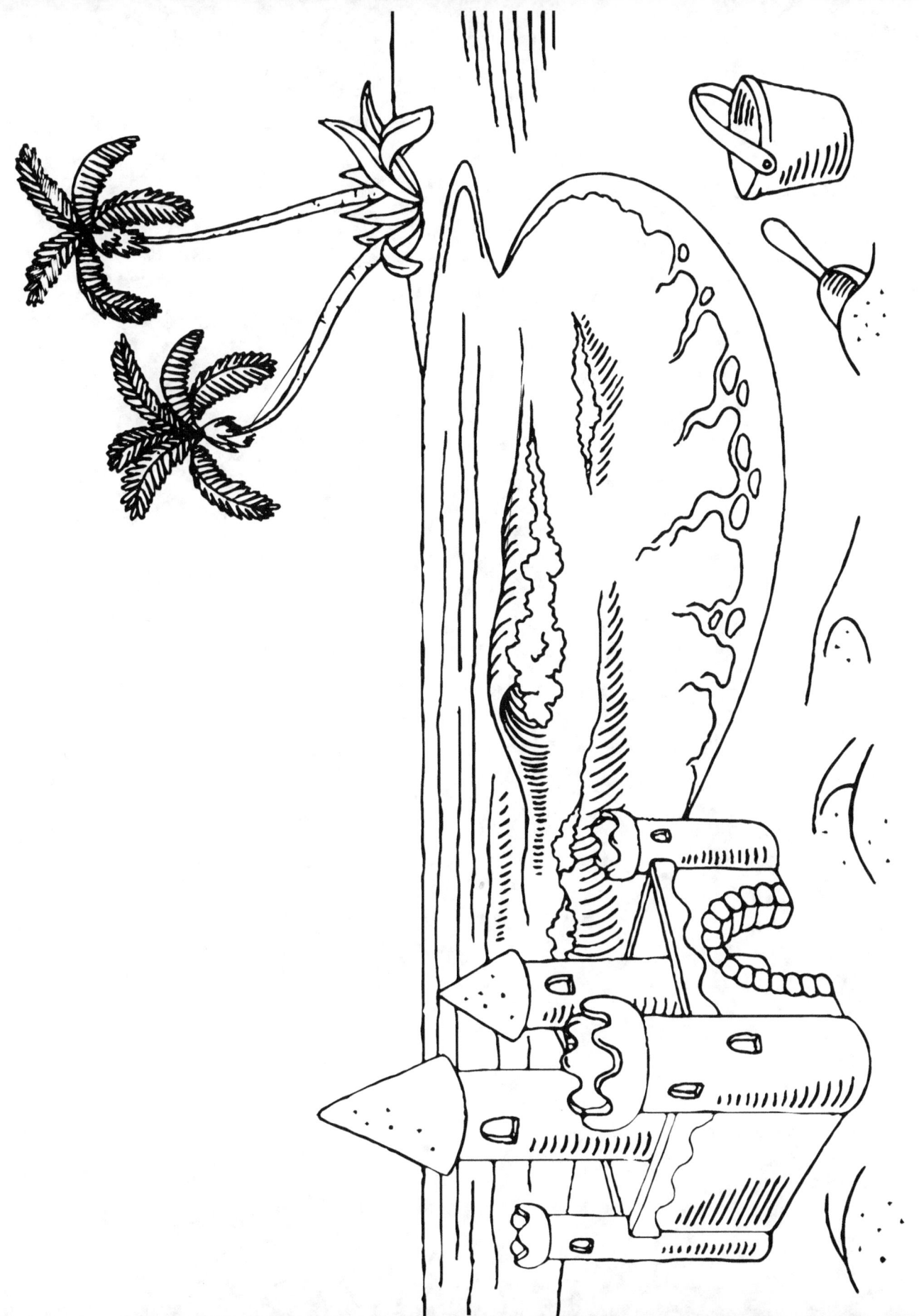

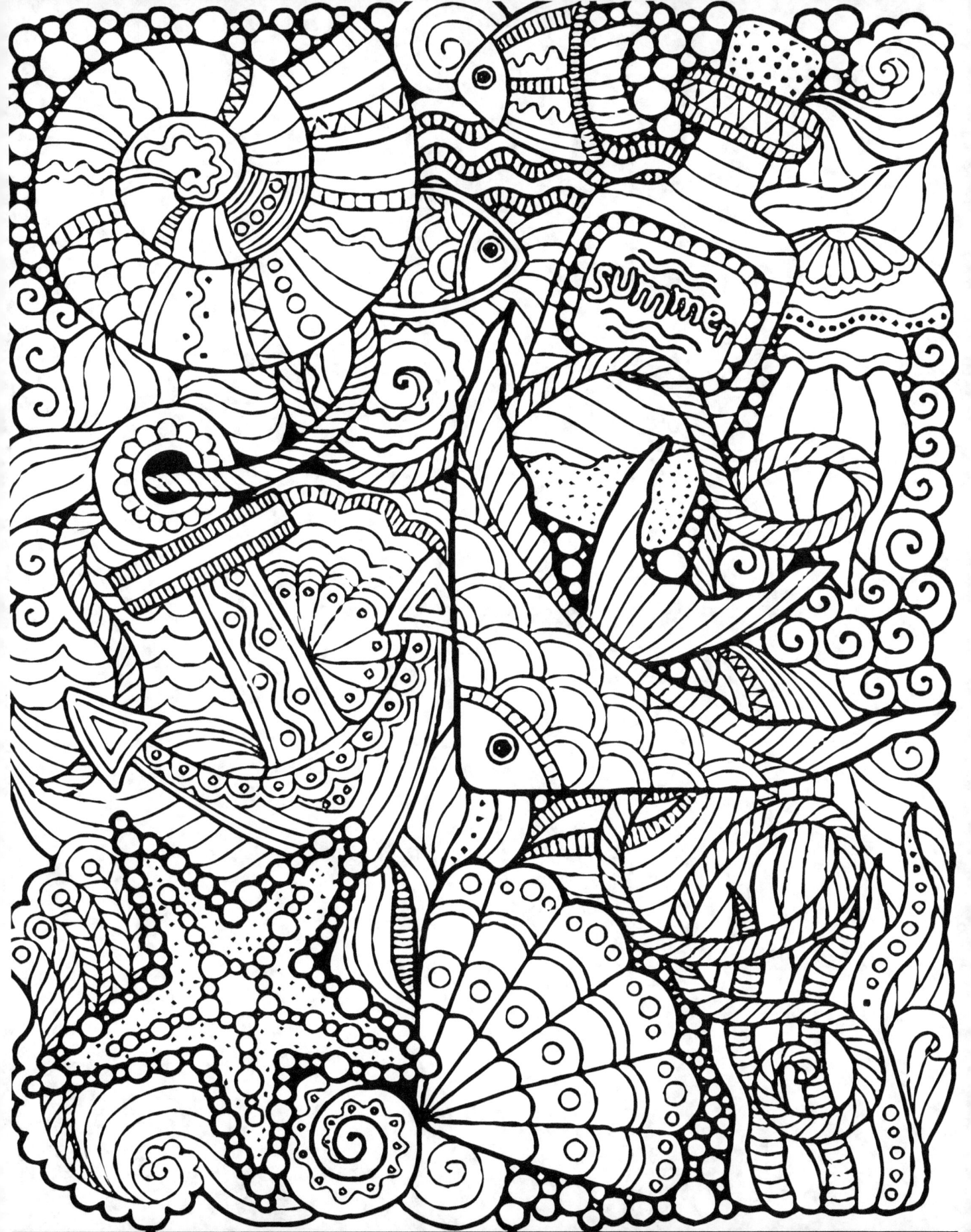

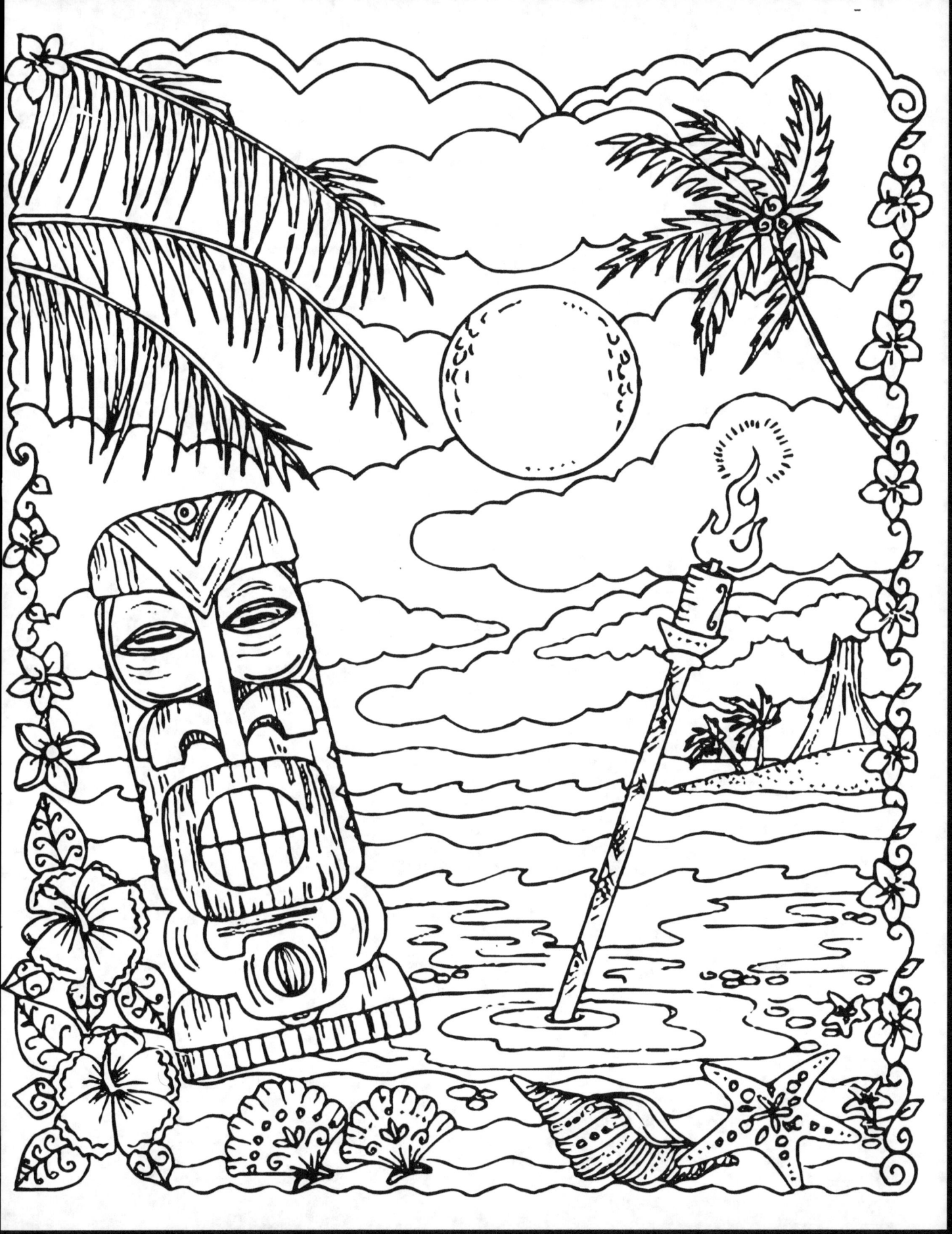

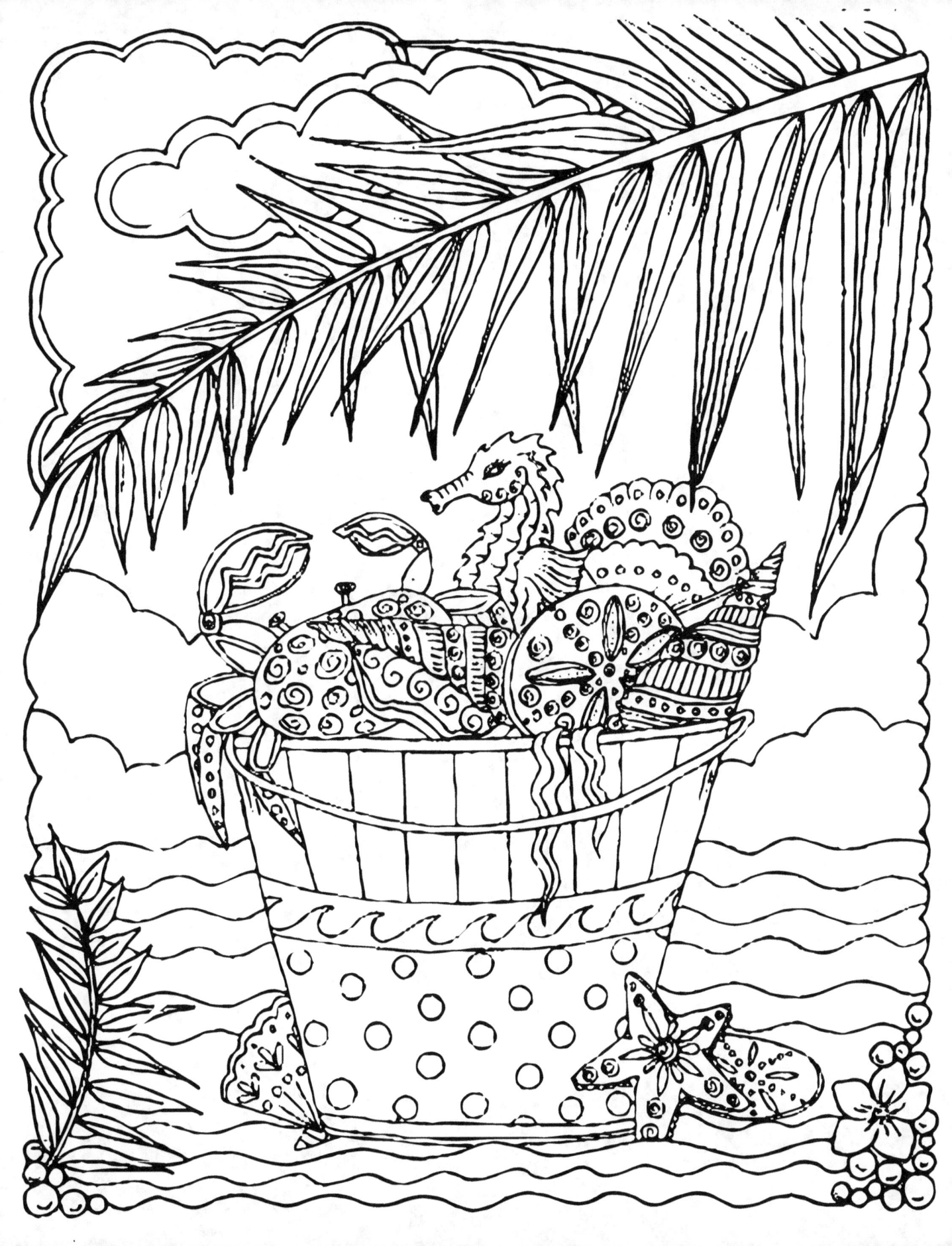

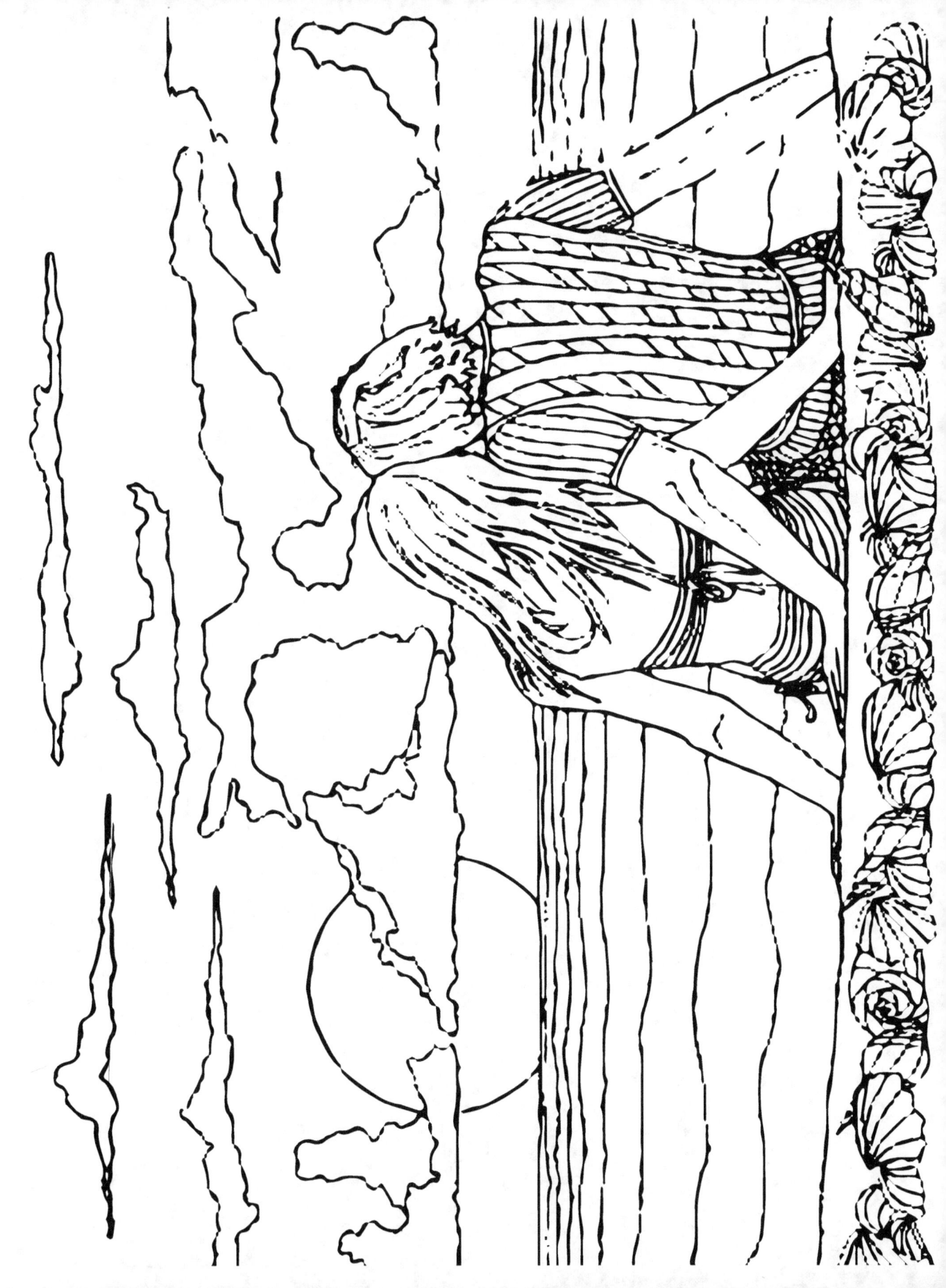

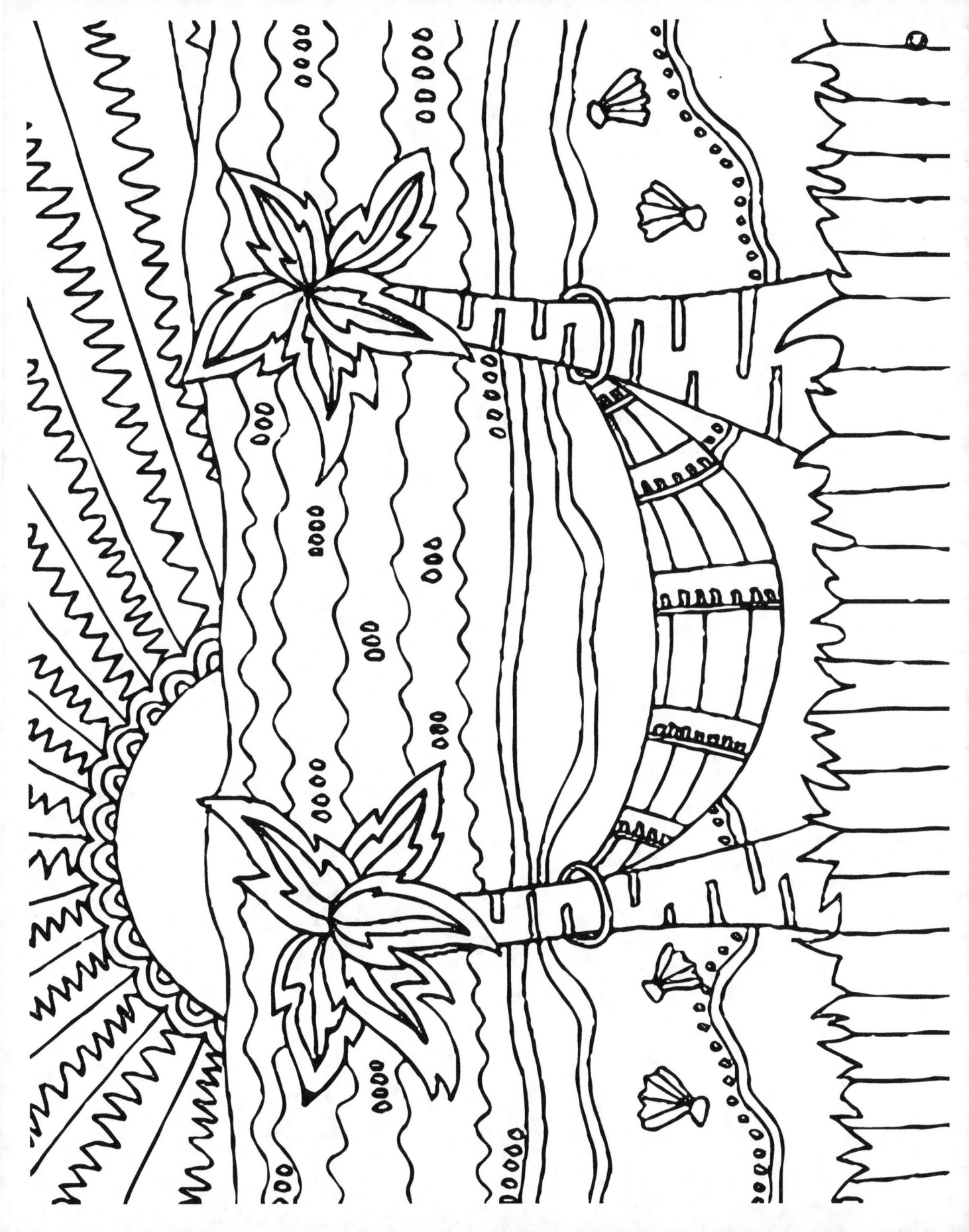

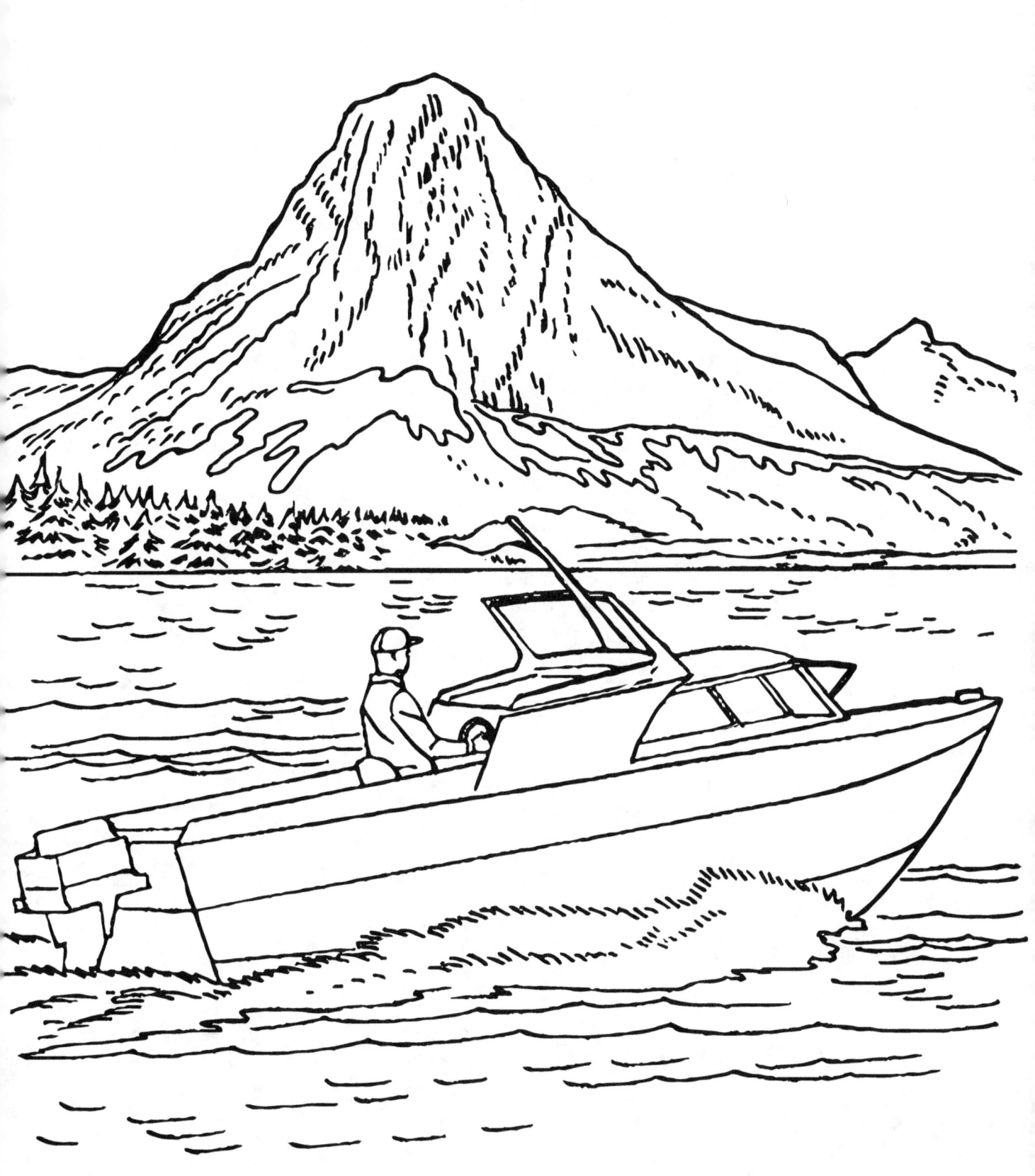

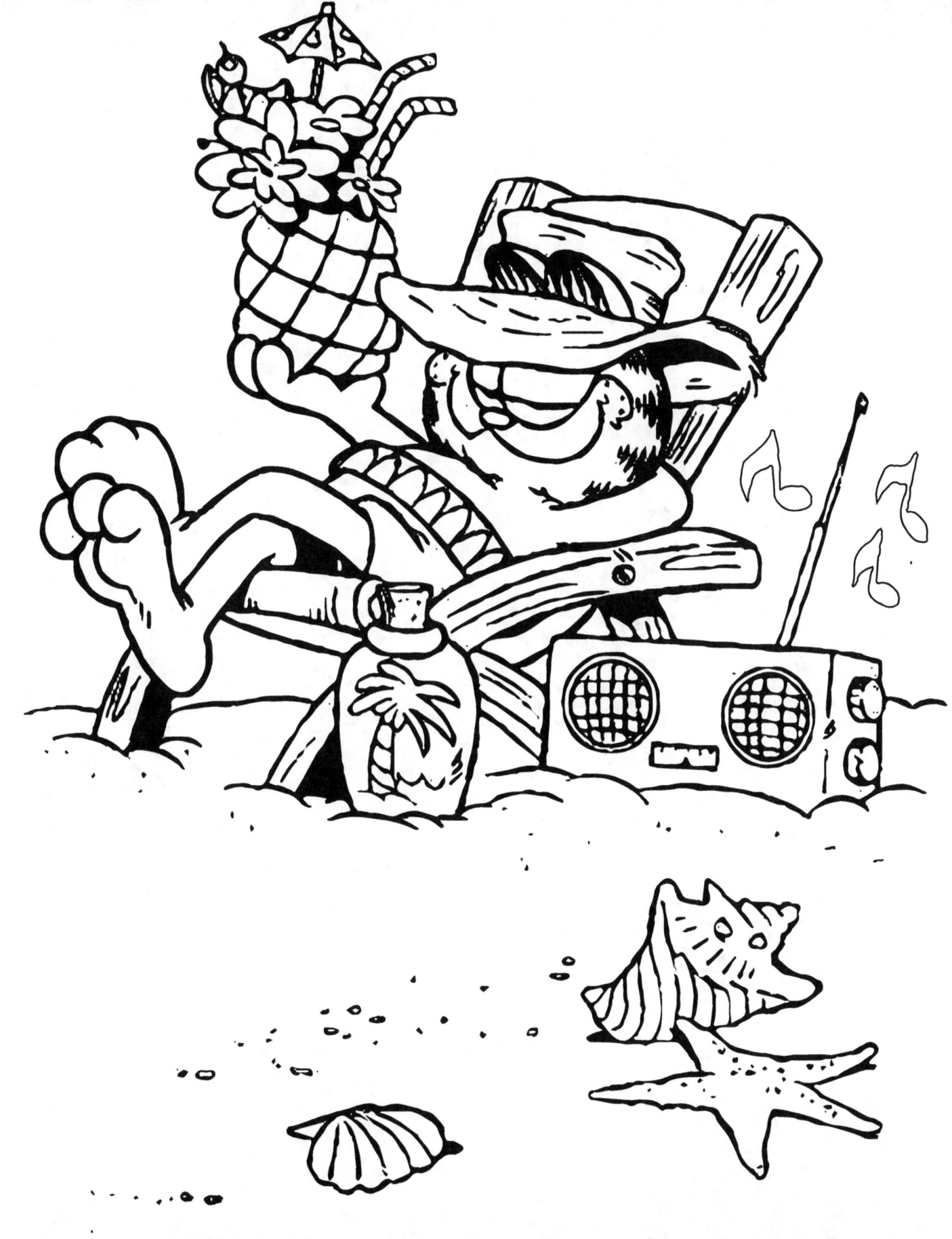

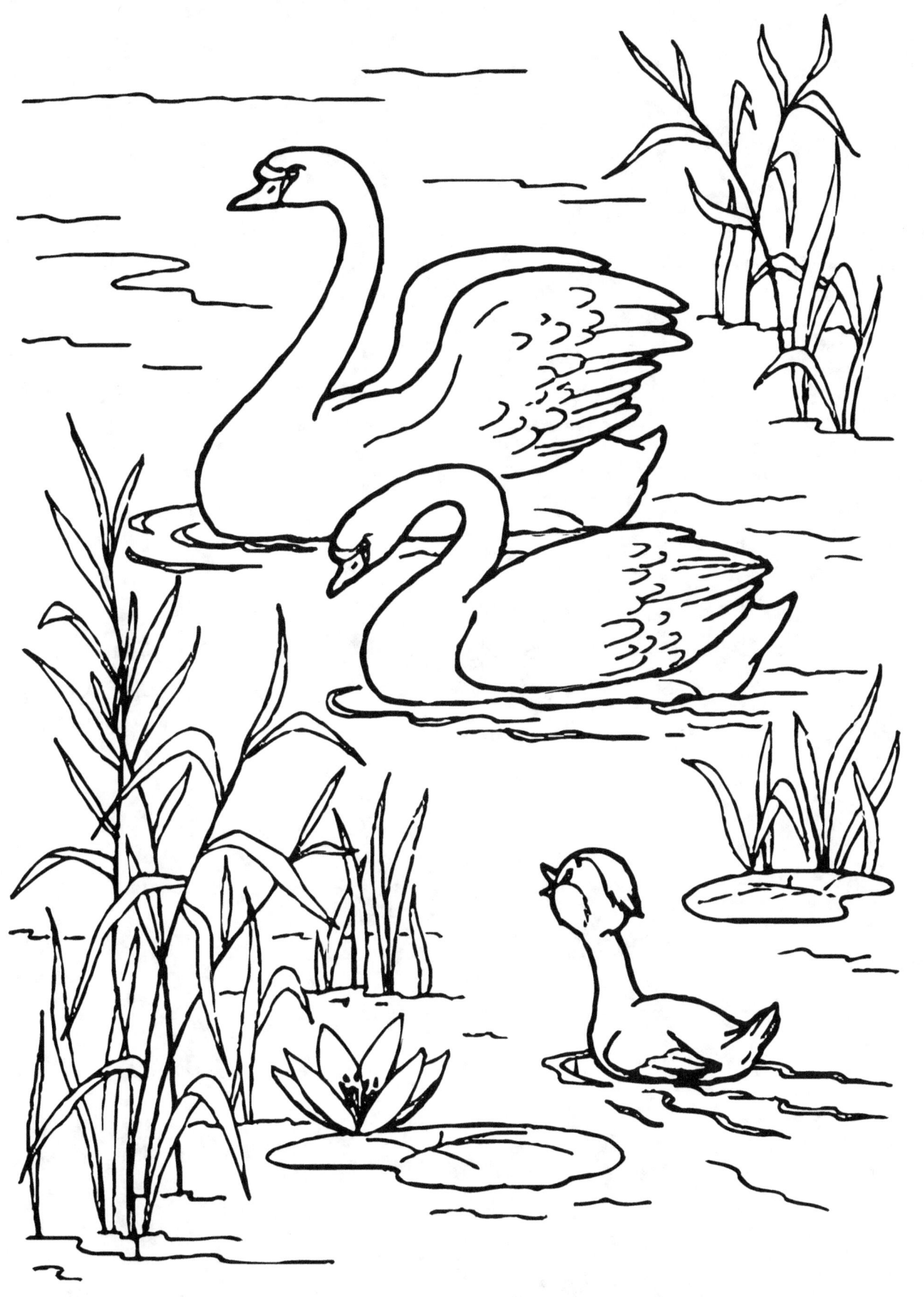

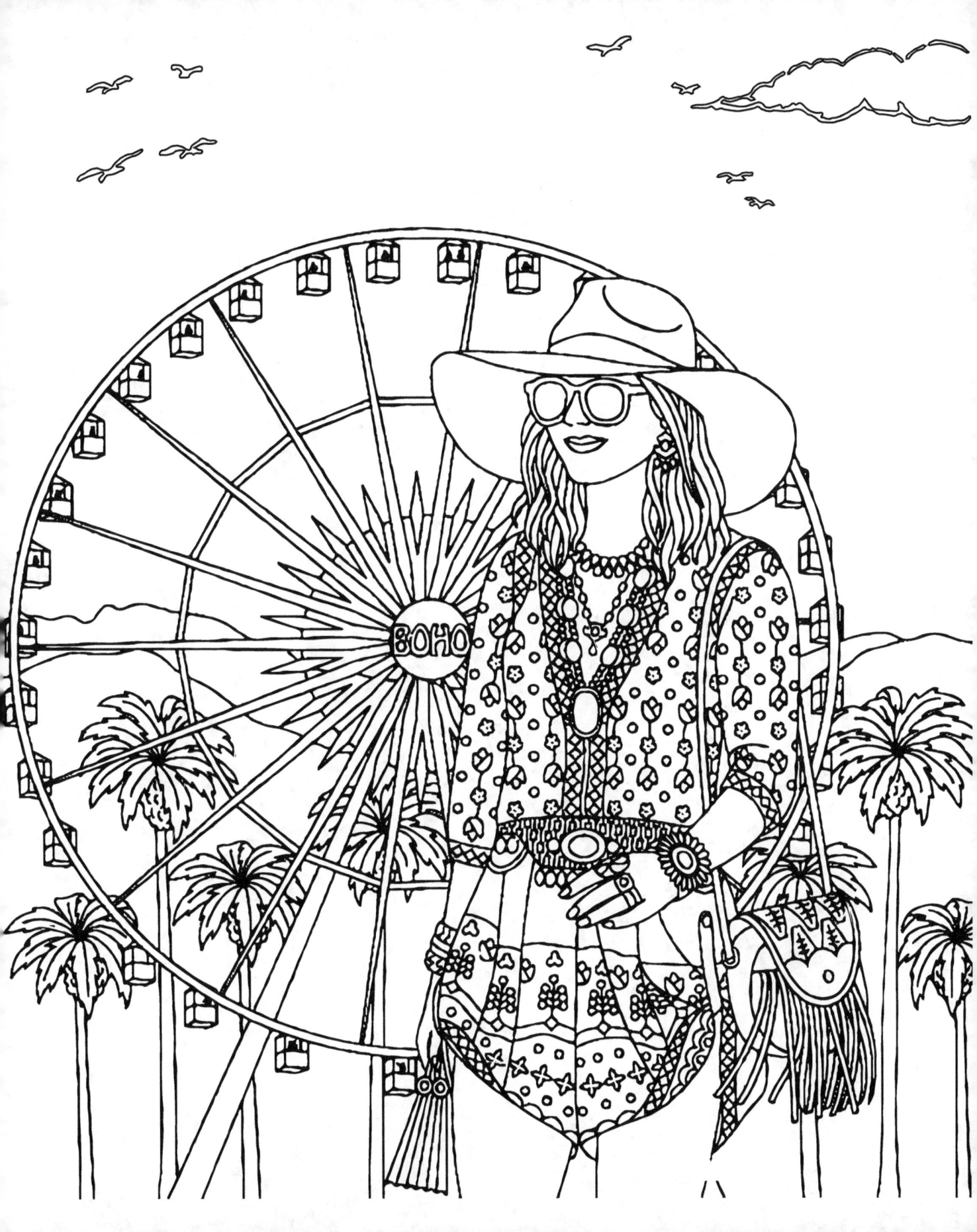

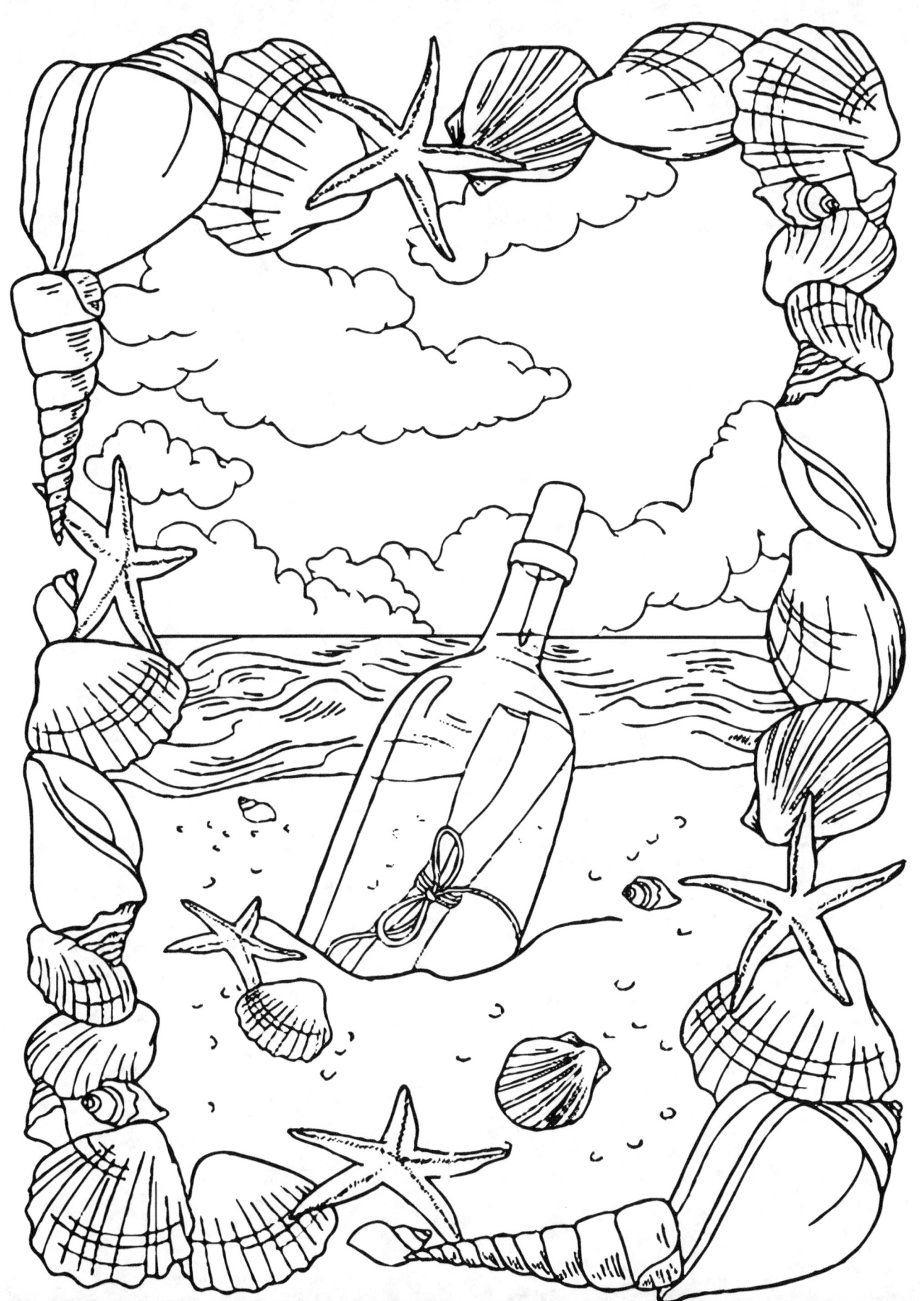

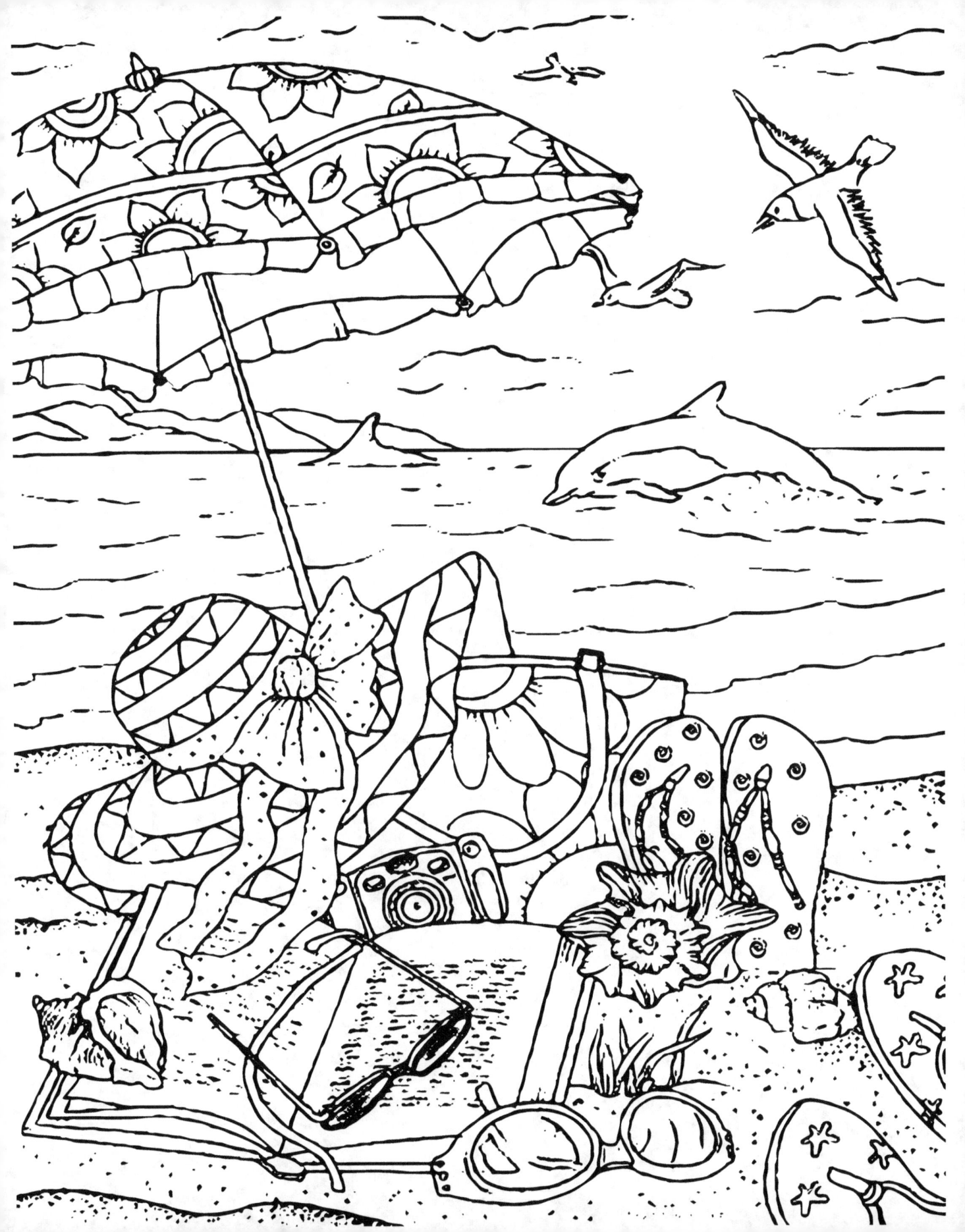

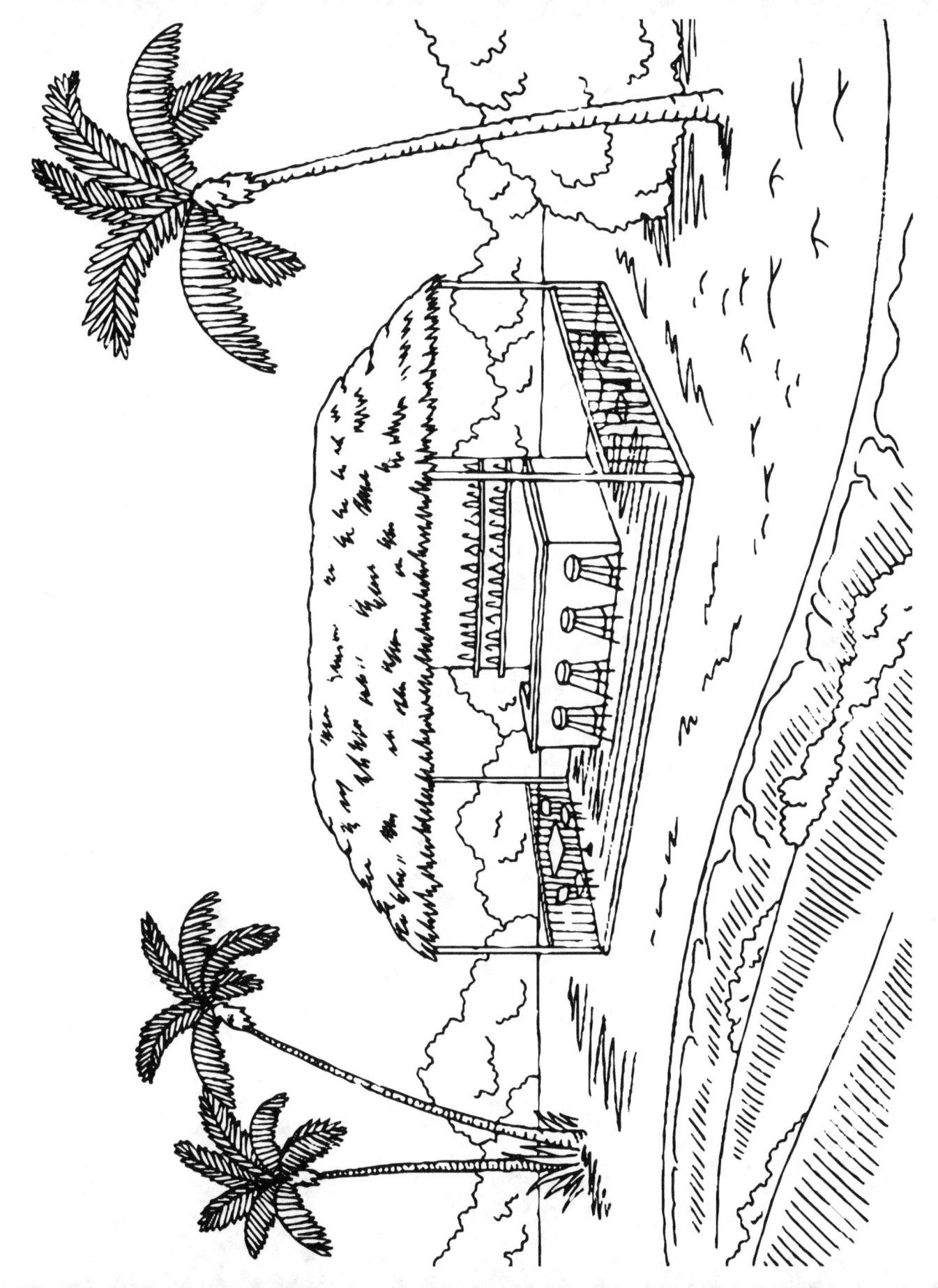

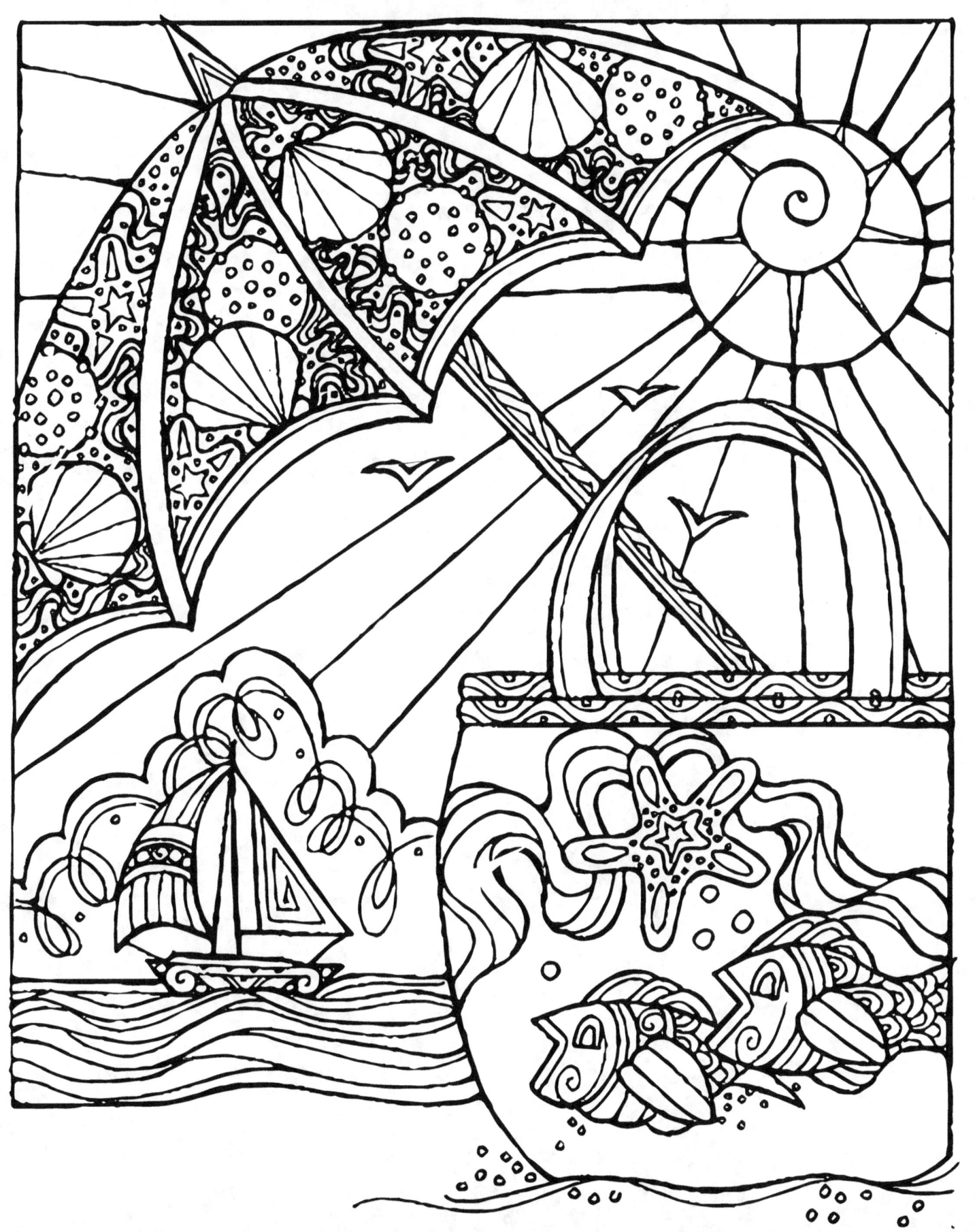

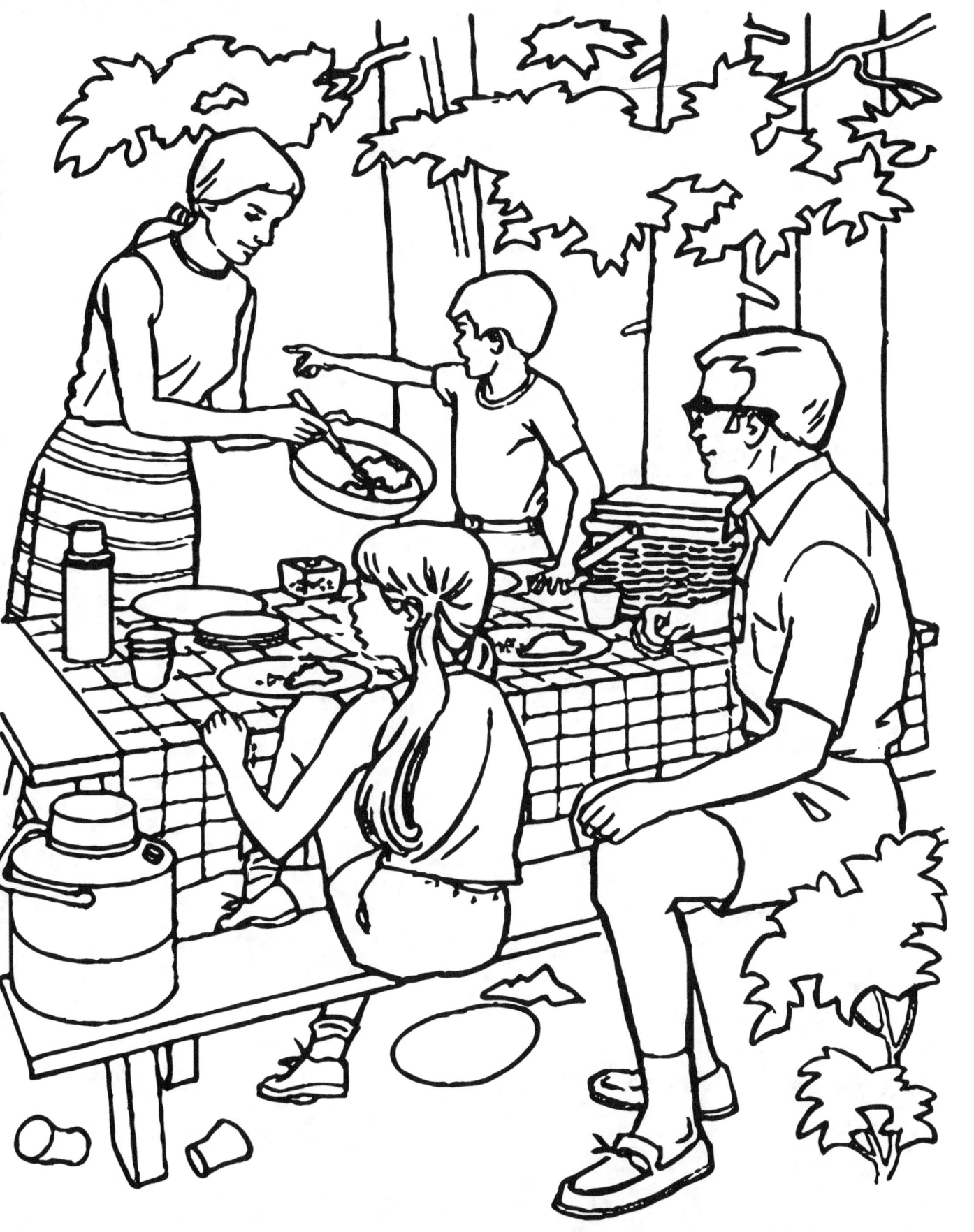

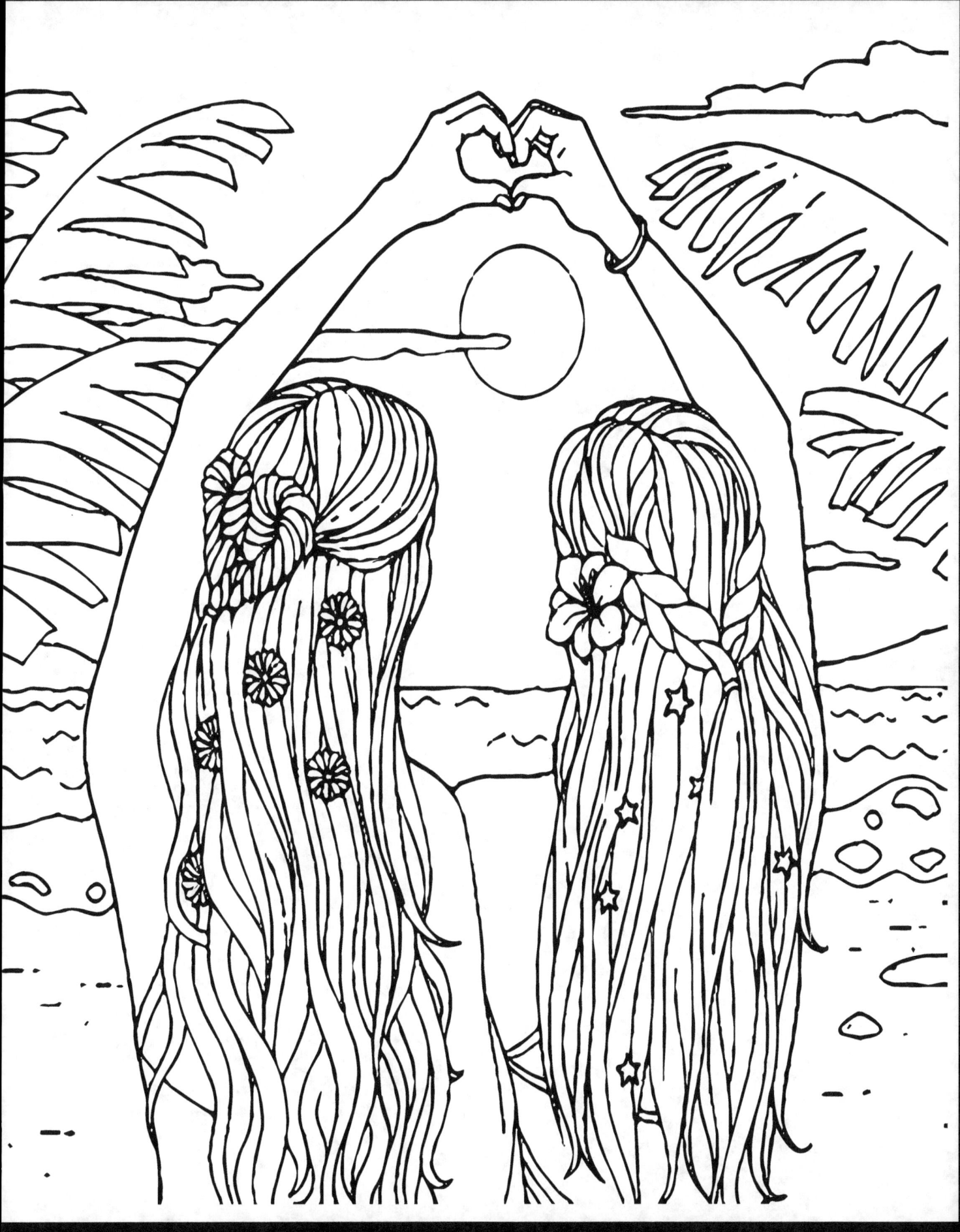

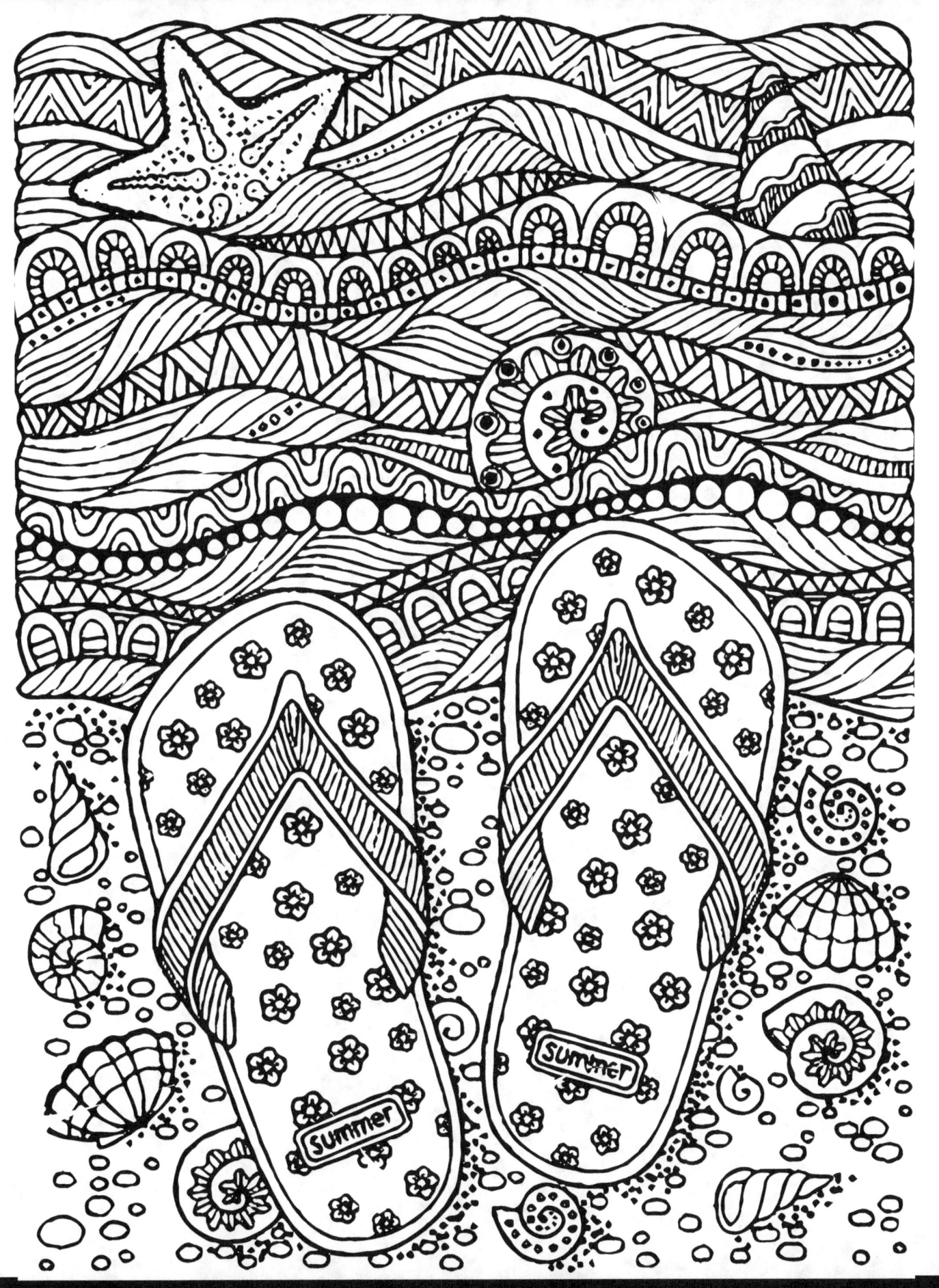

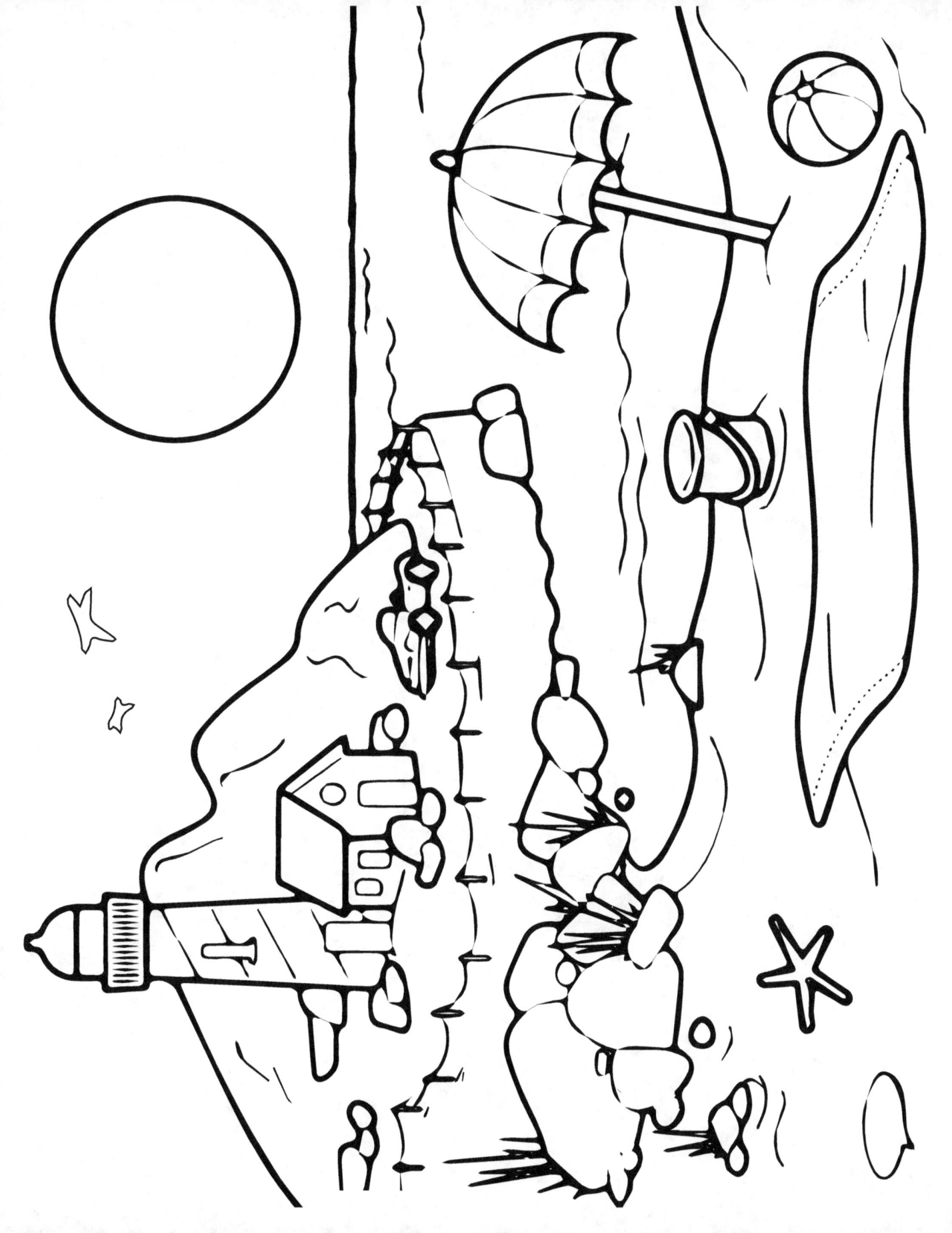

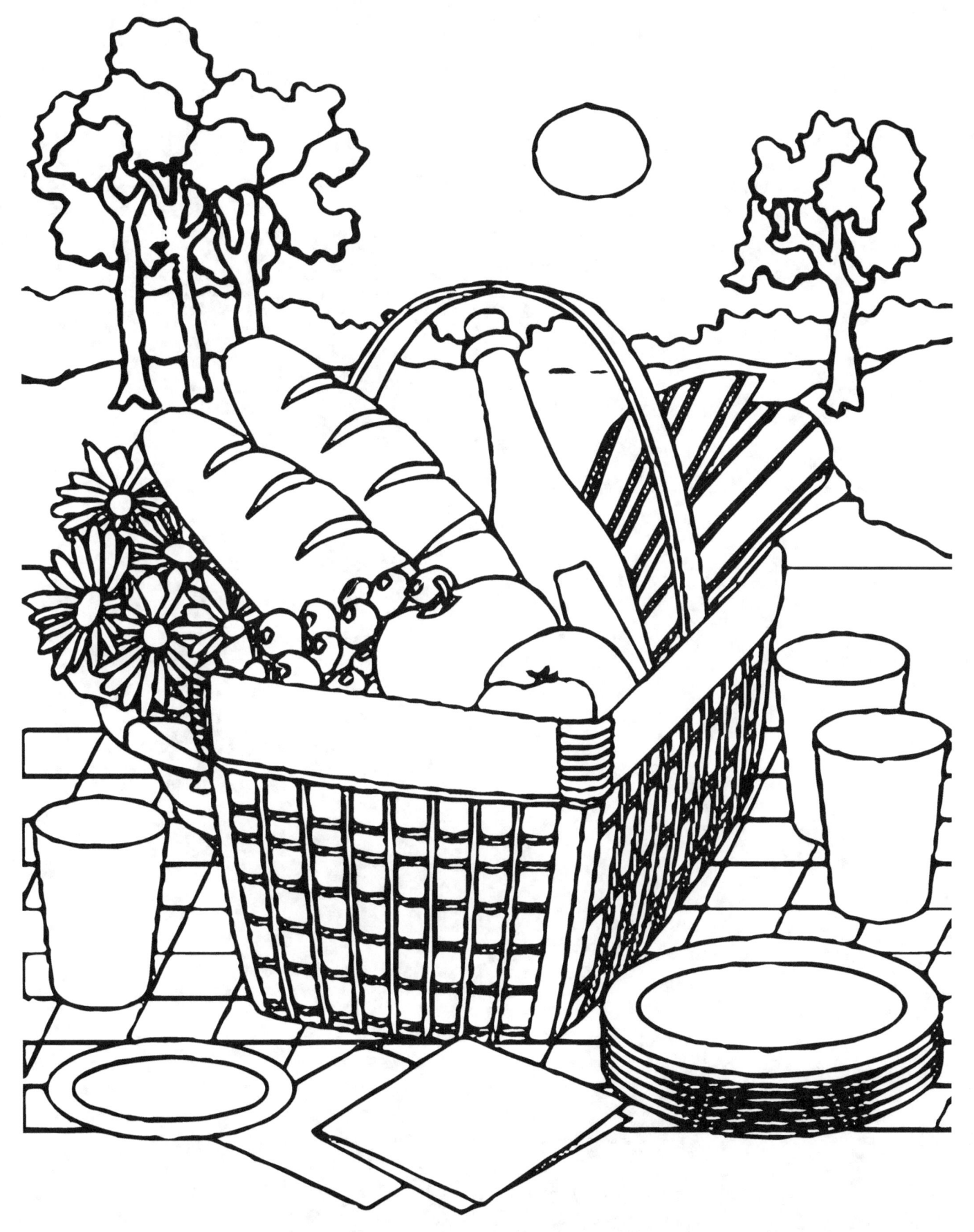

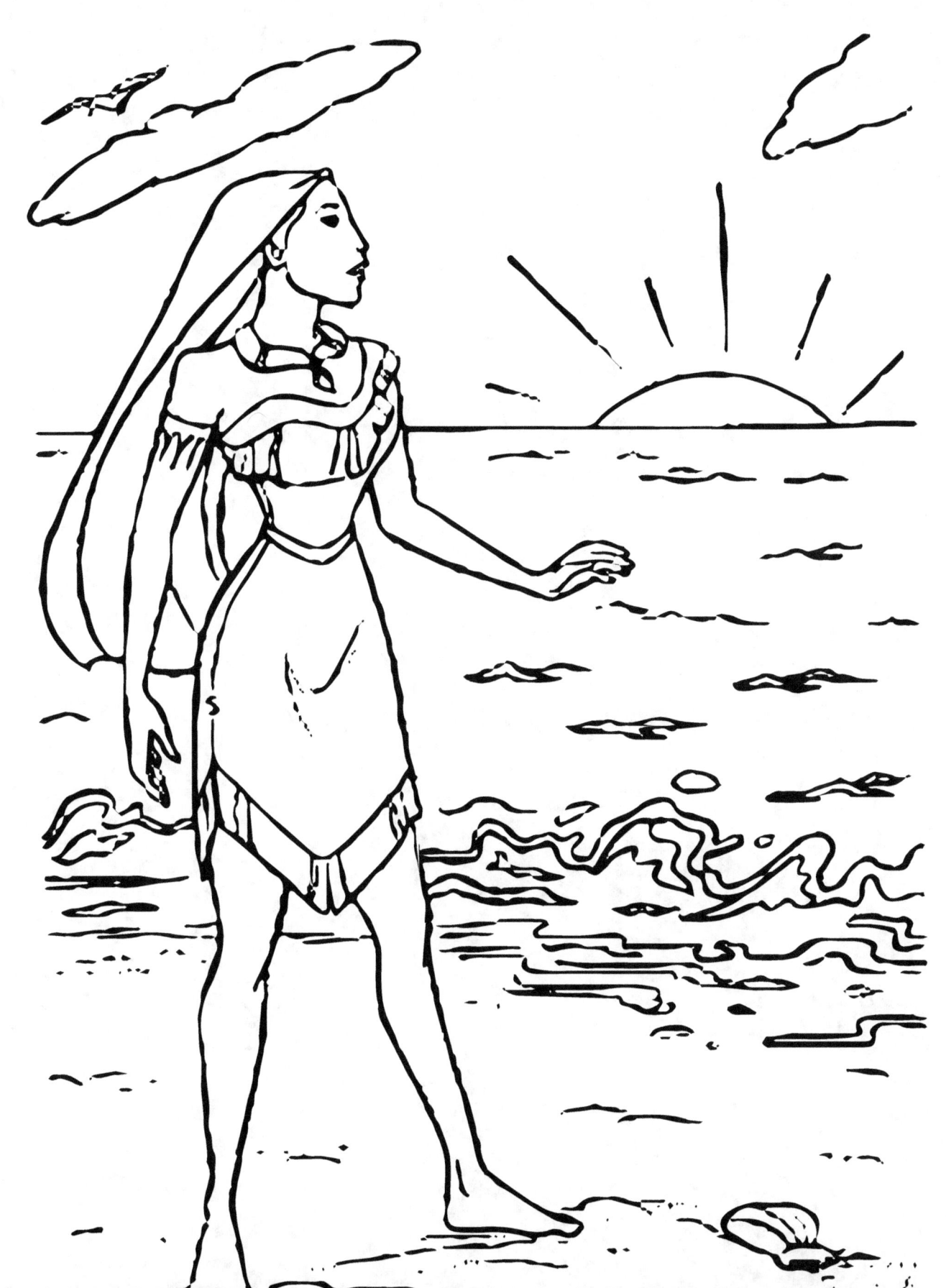

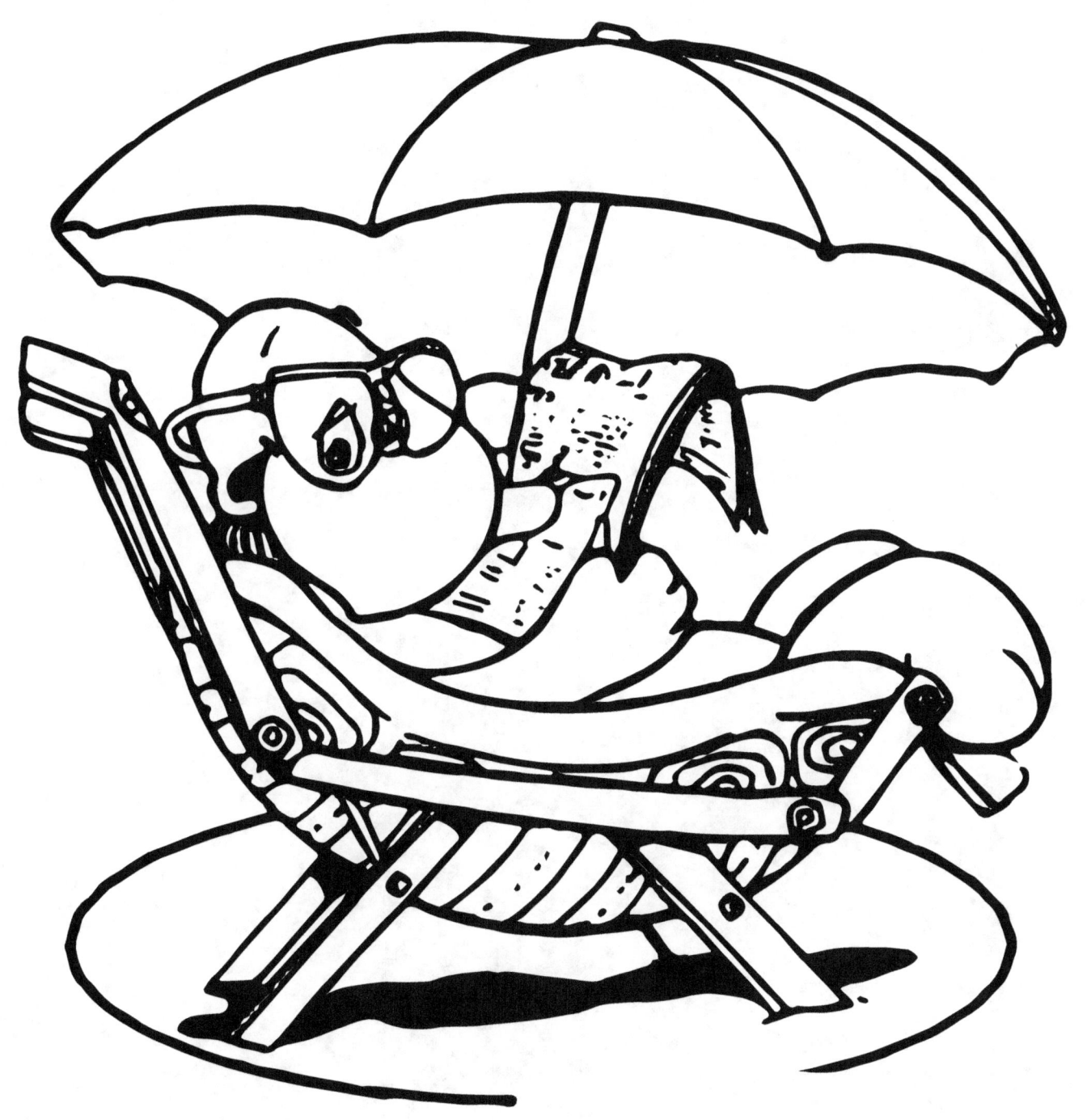

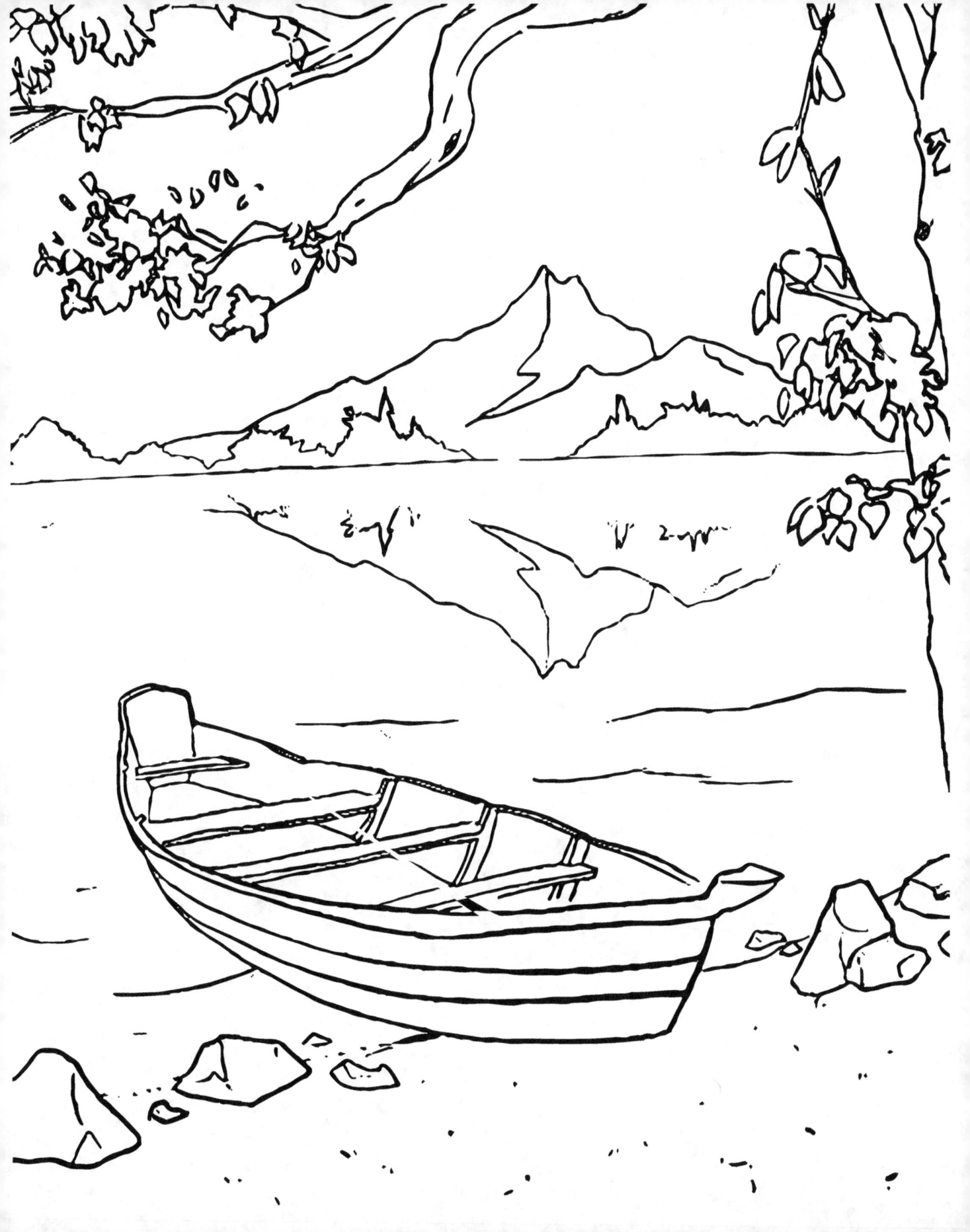

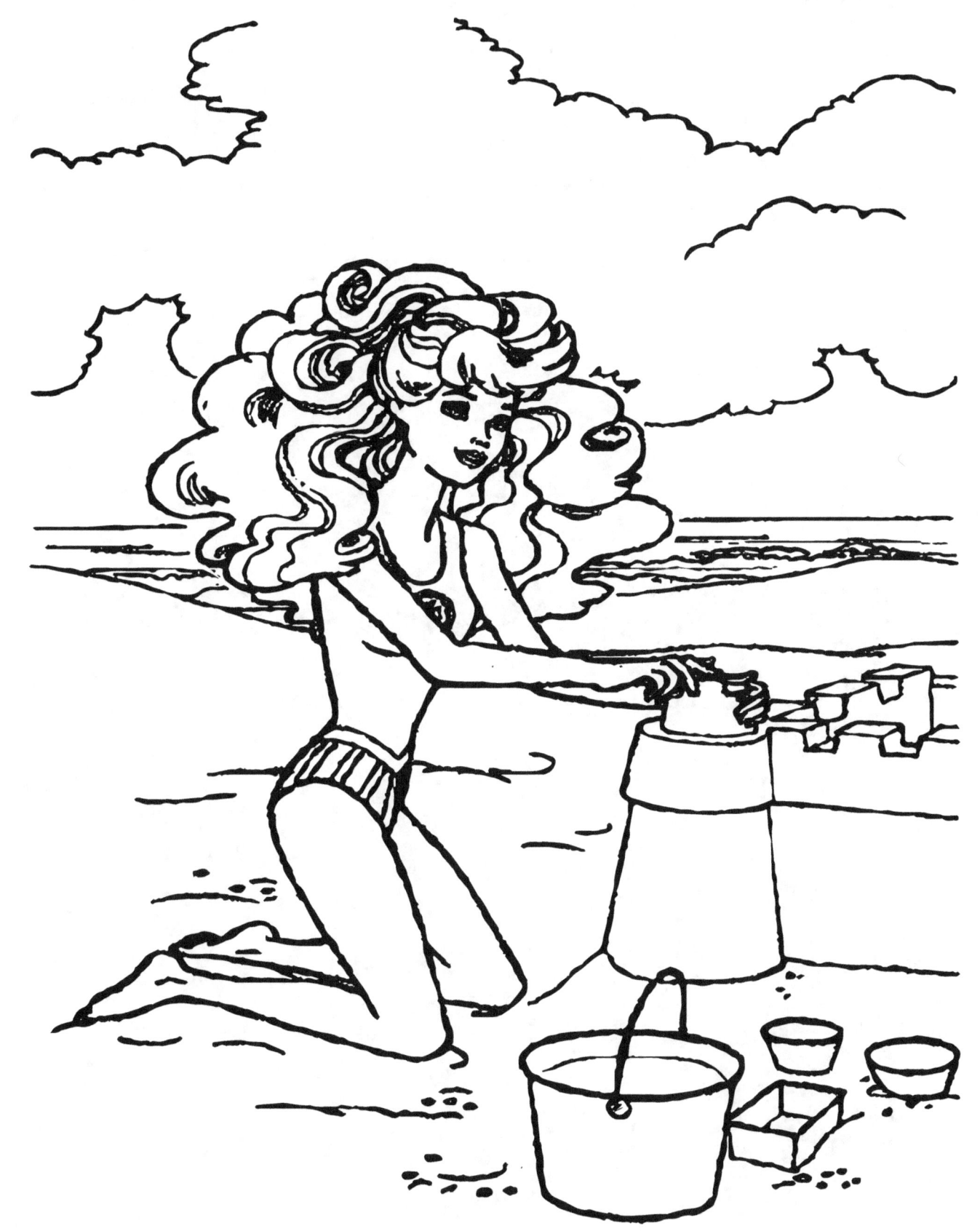

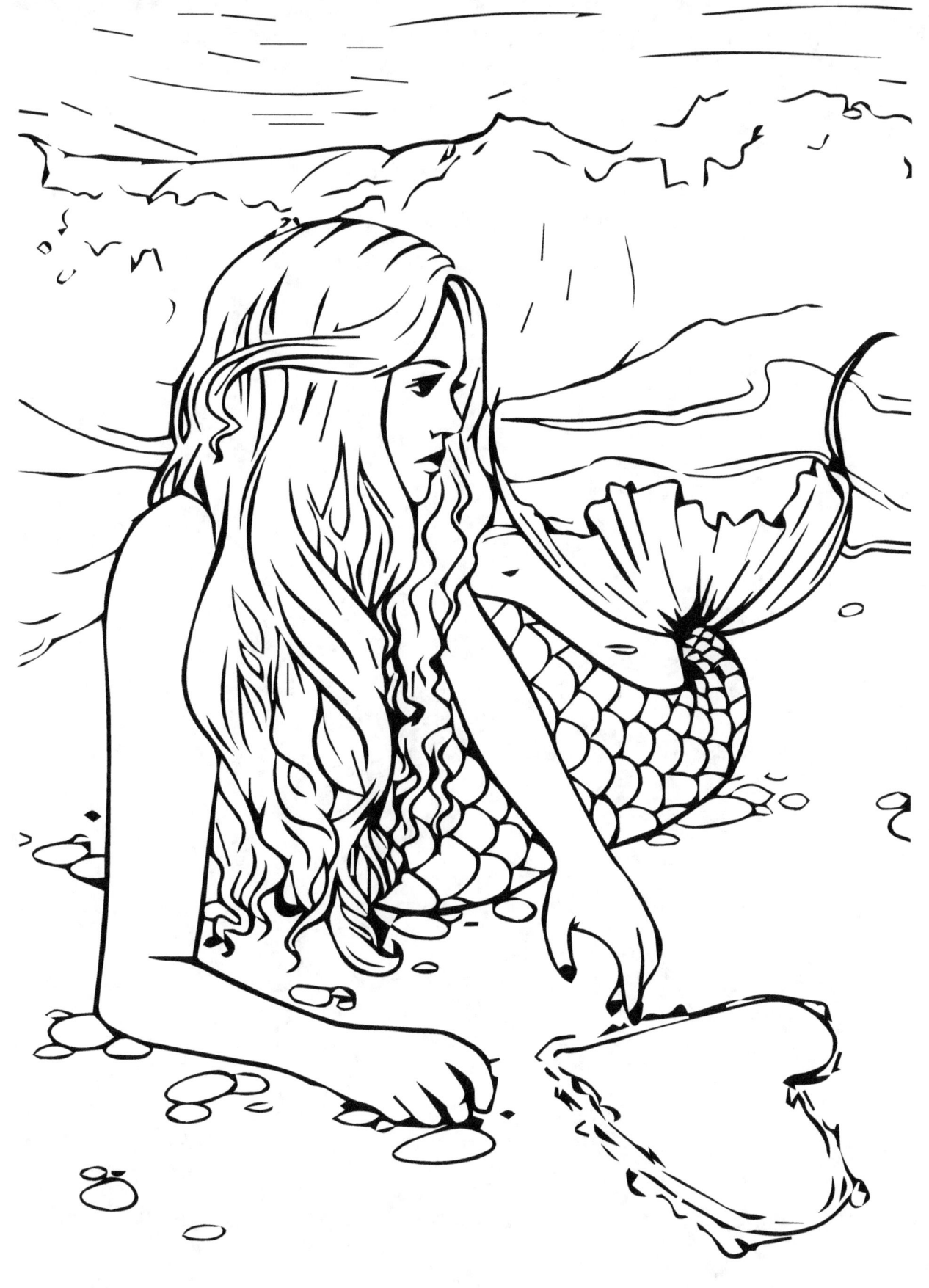

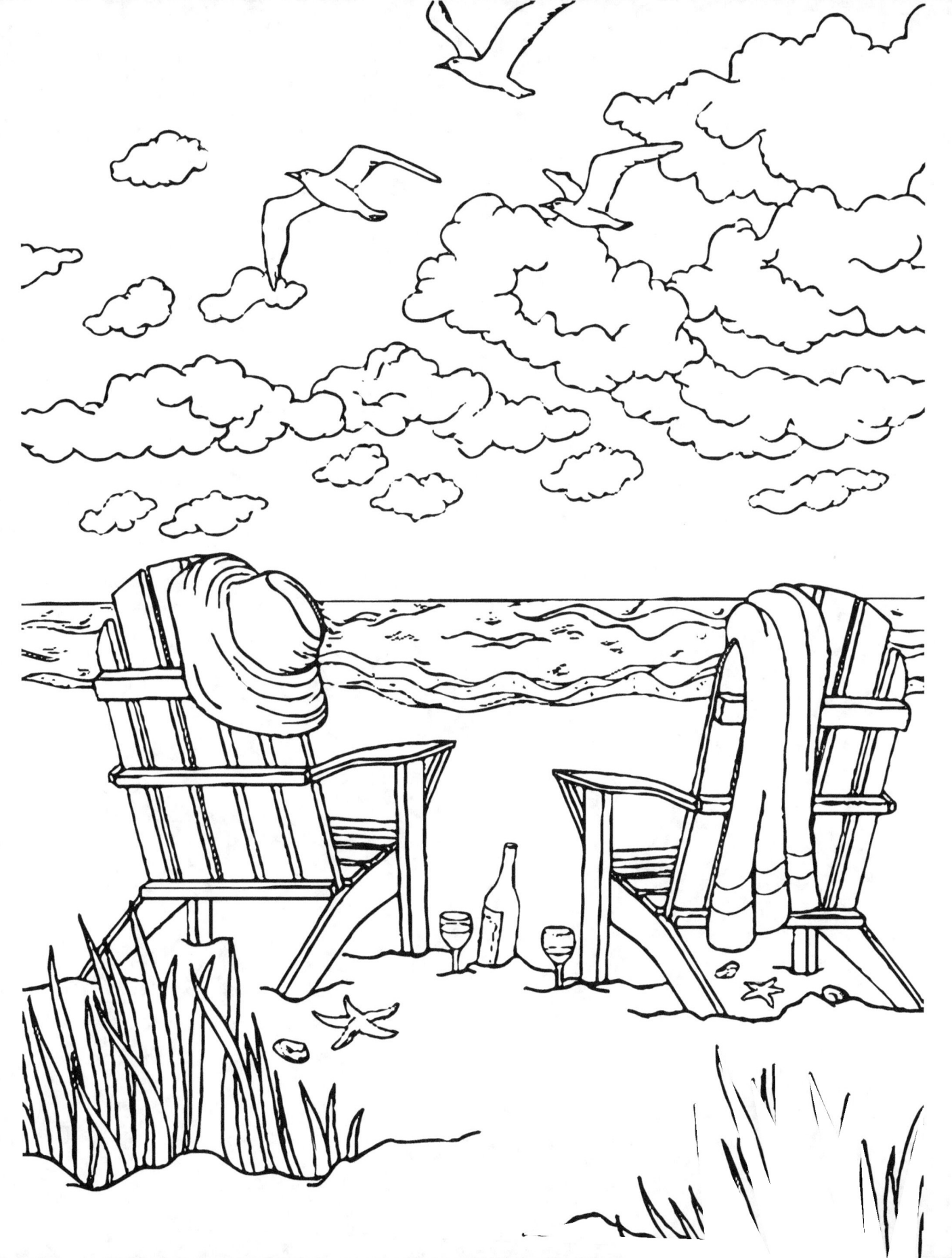

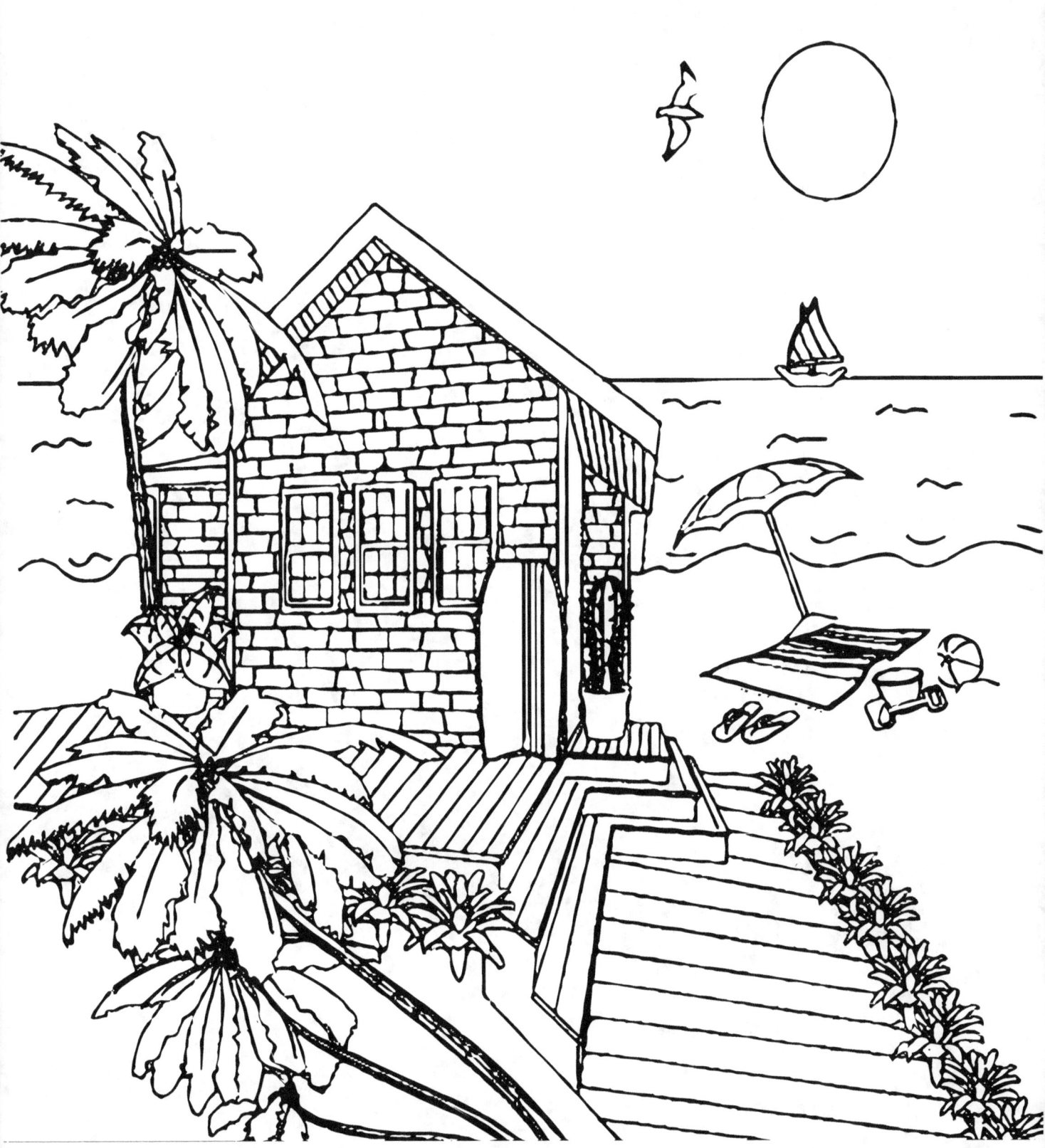

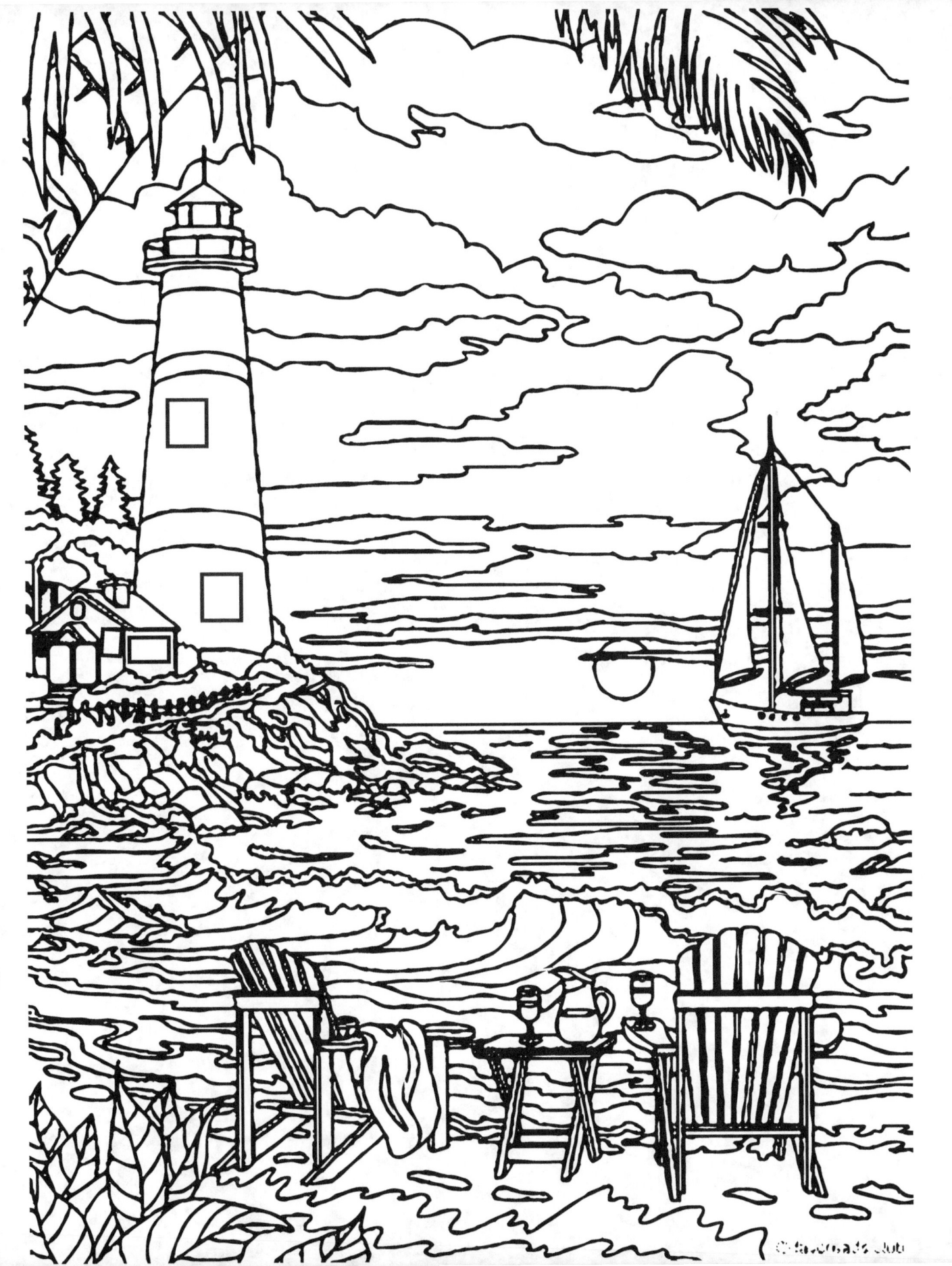

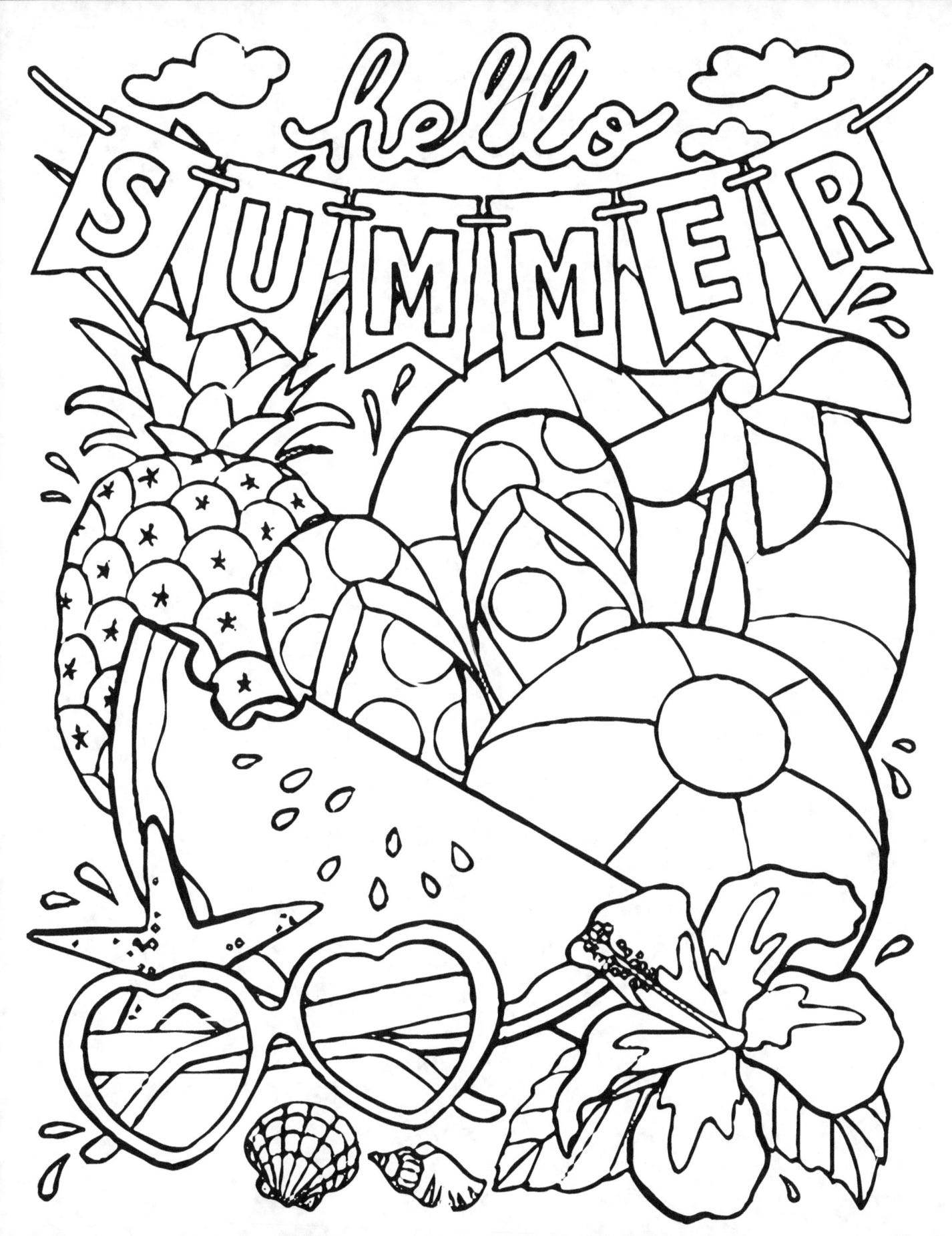

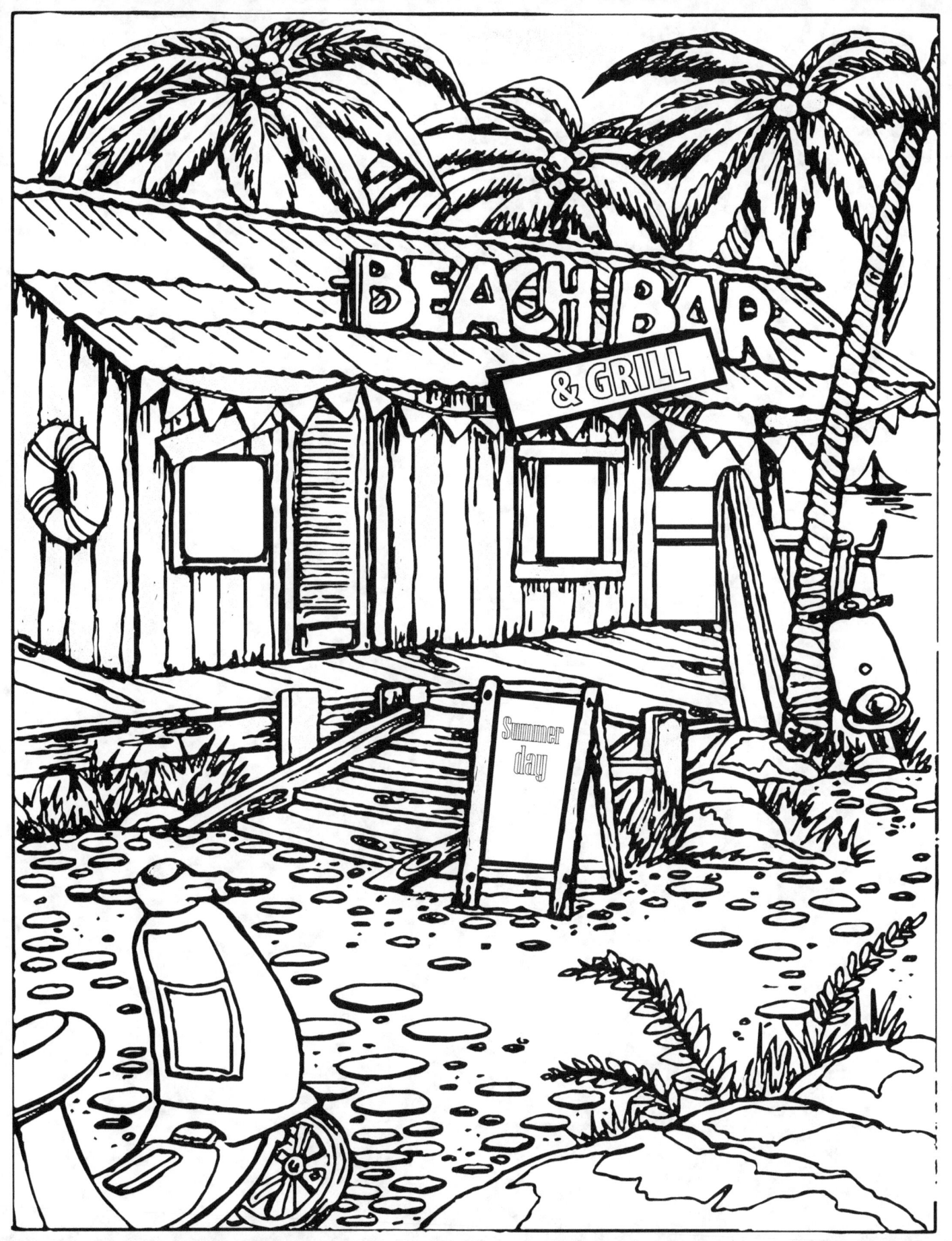

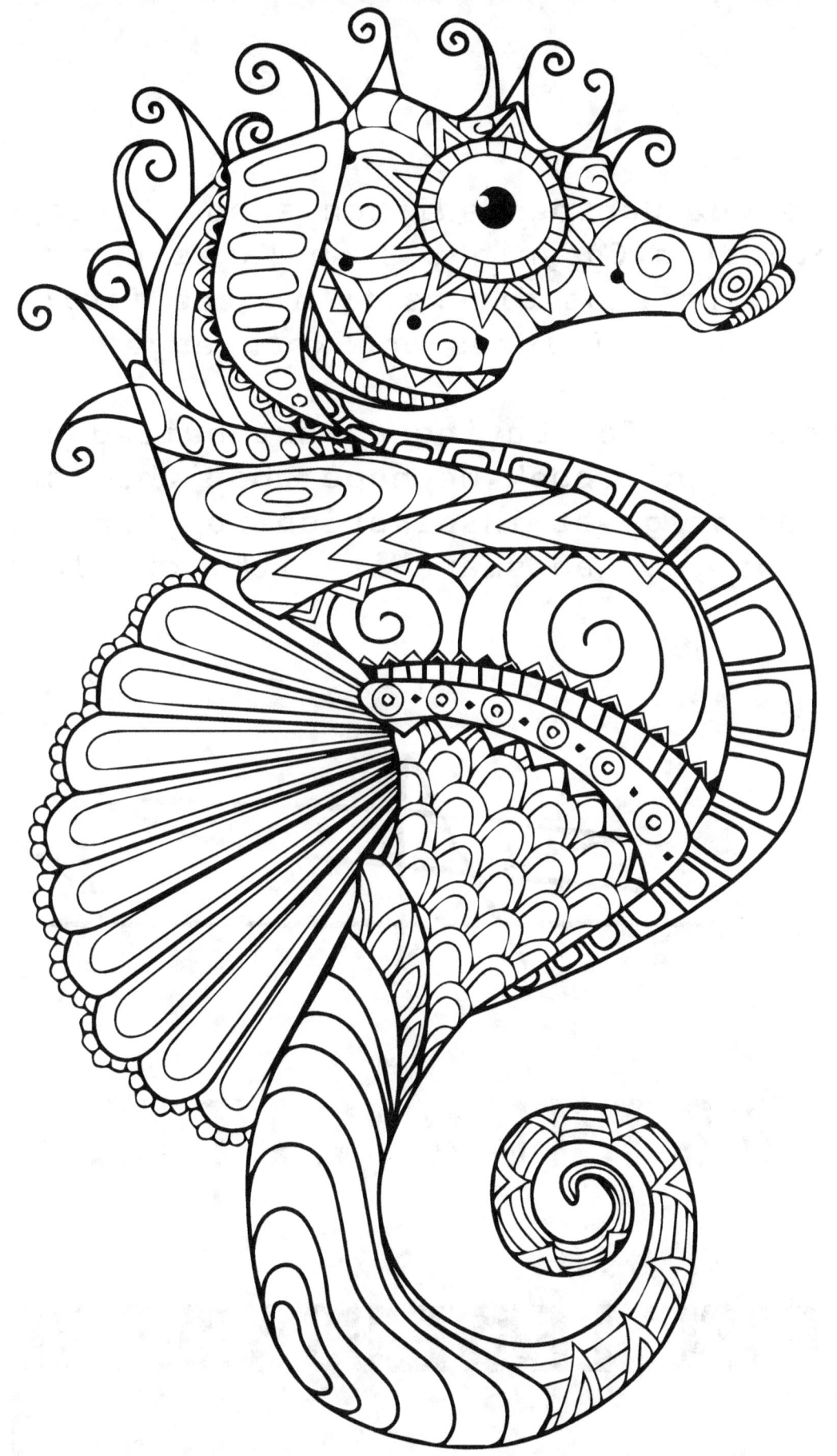

Invecruz Partner edition supports copyright protection. Copyright stimulates creativity, defends diversity in the field of ideas and knowledge.

Thank you for buying an authorized edition of this book. We hope that this book can be of great inspiration to your children, and that you can share it with your loved ones.

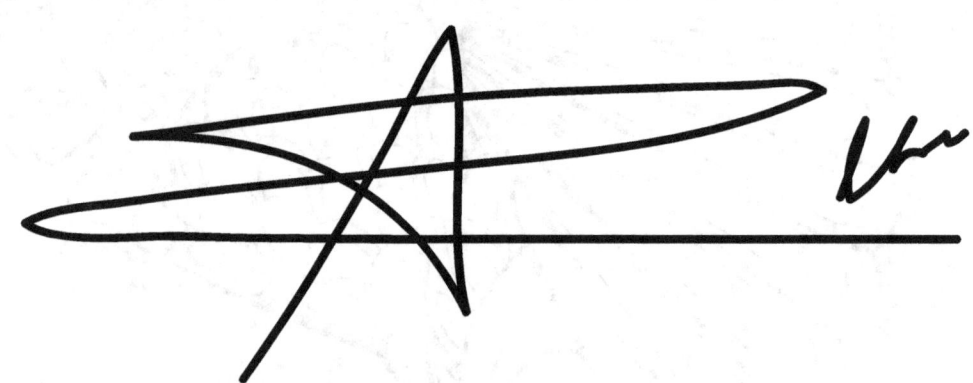

ARTHUR LITTLE

PLEASE LEAVE US YOUR REVIEW

www.ingramcontent.com/pod-product-compliance
Lightning Source LLC
Chambersburg PA
CBHW060437220526
45465CB00008B/3170